sail away

MICHAEL FRIEDEL
PHOTOGRAPHS THE
STAR CLIPPERS

WITH WORDS BY
WOLFGANG LIMMER

DEUTSCHER DSV. SPORTVERLAG

Logbook

Name of ship:

Year of construction:

Rig:

Type of construction:

Length overall:

Waterline length:

Beam:

Draught:

Sail area:

Engine:

Captain:

Crew:

Trip:

Day 1

Day 2

Day 3

Day 4

Day 5

Day 6

Day 7

Day 8

STAR FLYER

The Star Flyer takes her passengers through the Mediterranean, the cradle of western civilisation, and through the strange island world of the Andaman Sea, between India and Thailand. Twice a year the luxurious four-masted barquentine passes through the Suez Canal and cruises the Indian Ocean.

STAR CLIPPER

Since the early 1990s the sister-ship of the Star Flyer has been cruising through the varied seascapes of the Caribbean and the Mediterranean. The Star Clipper takes part in the annual Antigua Classic Yacht Regatta and ends the Caribbean season with one of the great trips under sail: crossing the Atlantic to the Mediterranean.

ROYAL CLIPPER

The Royal Clipper's design is based on the legendary Preussen (the German name for Prussia), the greatest five-masted sailing-ship of all time, also known as the Queen of the Seas. The impressive square-rigger cruises for half the year in the Mediterranean and half in the Caribbean. Twice yearly her passengers can cross the Atlantic, blown by the trade-winds, just as in the days of Columbus.

CONTENTS

explanation of symbols:

➢ next double-page

Making drea

At the stroke of 1 p.m. on 28 July 2000, in Monte Carlo harbour, a bottle of champagne shattered on a ship's bow, just beneath a graceful figurehead with long, blond hair. It made a dream come true for a man who seems to combine as many extraordinary qualities as the commonplaces he personifies. One such commonplace is that your name is your destiny. The Swedish ship-owner Mikael Krafft had shown more than his share of strength (in German, *Kraft*) in working towards this moment. Queen Silvia of Sweden, »his« queen, had thrown the bottle of champagne that christened the ship, and his daughter Marie had modelled for the figurehead that adorned it. Since this christening, the ROYAL CLIPPER has also carried the honorary title of »Queen of the Seas«. She is, after all, the only five-masted sailing-ship on the world's oceans. With her, Krafft is reviving a long-lost seafaring tradition, whose mothballed relics in museums were among his most enduring childhood memories.

Born in Stockholm in 1946, Krafft was only ten when he was given his first little sailing-dinghy. In it, with neither a compass nor his parents' permission, he sailed out for 20 nautical miles across open sea, because he knew that in the Aaland islands, midway between Sweden and Finland, the German four-masted barque POMMERN, a floating museum, had tied up in the harbour of Mariehamn. The small boy was amazed when he boarded the vessel, built in Glasgow in 1902 for the Hamburg shipping firm of Wencke & Schöne. It dated from the legendary era of the »Flying P« windjammers, like the PREUSSEN and POMMERN, which voyaged between Europe, America and Asia at the beginning of the 20th century. Young Mikael studied the square-rigger in detail, and since his parents lived near a shipyard, he got the men who worked there to tell him pretty much everything there was to know about the clipper-ships and their brilliant designers. The one who impressed him most was the Scottish-American ship-builder, Donald McKay. The tea-clippers he designed and built in Boston at the end of the 19th century are considered to this day by sailing-ship experts to be unsurpassed in speed and elegance. They and the POMMERN would later serves as models for Krafft when building his own fleet. For that was the dream of the little boy in his dinghy – to bring alive once more the world of those legendary ships.

Once the sea has someone in its grasp, it never lets go. Krafft set off on his journey with iron determination. In Sweden and Geneva he studied international law and the law of the sea, and after graduating with honours he became an advisor to Swedish shipping companies. By the age of thirty he was already the managing partner in a small ship-owning firm. At that time it was embroiled in a complicated legal wrangle with the Japanese Hitachi group. Krafft succeeded in resolving the deadlock and helped the shipping firm to achieve considerable growth. At the age of forty, Mikael Krafft sold his shares in the company and moved to Brussels. He took a six-month vacation and sailed the world's oceans in his yacht GLORIA, until he realised he was not cut out for a life of leisure. Krafft is a man of action, a

ms come true

shaper of events, not an observer; a man who took his pilot's licence because he has to fly a lot and likes to be at the controls himself. So, when he was 42, he set up a group of companies in Brussels, whose maritime centrepiece is the cruise-line, Star Clippers Inc., based in Miami. At the start, just two dozen people worked there, and Krafft's first undertaking was to build the two barquentines, STAR FLYER (May 1991) and STAR CLIPPER (April 1992). The design of both these 4-masted ships was based on the blueprints of the brilliant Donald McKay, which Krafft had studied in detail when still in his teens. »In those days I knew more about clippers than about women,« Krafft admits today.

He invested a total of $80 million in building and fitting out these two ships, which were intended to attract a market of sports-minded tourists, seeking the challenges of seamanship. From a survey of some 3,000 cruise passengers, Krafft had discovered that this market existed. The respondents revealed something he called »mega-yacht syndrome« – a »disease« that he had certainly succumbed to himself – and one that forms the key psychological factor in his formula for success. This syndrome is a well-balanced blend of nostalgia for the romance of old-fashioned sailing in the world's most beautiful waters, the need for luxury and the urge for athletic activity – from water-skiing, through scuba-diving to active participation in regattas. And all this was to be offered at affordable prices. With typical thoroughness Krafft turned the concept into reality, taking care of every detail, even sailing on a cruise himself, to study what his passengers wanted and what they were getting – and he achieved instant success. Today the number of people actively employed in his cruise business is around 450.

Then in 2000 he built the ROYAL CLIPPER, a unique sailing-ship in every respect, and one that brings back to life all those images from his childhood, when he secretly crept aboard the POMMERN and blithely promised himself that one day he would own a vessel like that. The ROYAL CLIPPER is in fact several metres longer than the POMMERN and has one more mast. The design for the clipper was modelled on the PREUSSEN, the only fully square-rigged five-masted ship of its day to sail the high seas in the era of the last windjammers. She made her maiden voyage on 31 July 1902, for the famous Hamburg shipping company, Laeisz. With a vast cargo capacity of 8,000 tons, her sail-area of over 5,560 square metres gave her a maximum speed of 21 knots.

So now the PREUSSEN was to rise again in new and more luxurious splendour. In a Polish shipyard Krafft had discovered an iron hull that was intended for a Soviet sail-training ship. The Polish marine architect Zygmunt Choren fitted it with a new, more elegant bow and a multi-functional stern, from which a sports-platform can be raised and lowered hydraulically.

Everywhere you can see the hand of the ship-owner, who has turned his vision into reality. And for him the finest compliment is the saying commonly heard among sailors: there are three ways to sail – the wrong way, the right way, and the Star Clippers way.

2000
ROYAL CLIPPE

STAR CLIPPERS

The ROYAL CLIPPER leaving Marigot bay, St Lucia.

The ROYAL CLIPPER under full sail off Soufriere, St Lucia.

The ROYAL CLIPPER leaving Marigot bay, St Lucia.

Looking aloft at the ROYAL CLIPPER'S square-sails and jib..

The bridge of the ROYAL CLIPPER, with St George's, Grenada, in the background.

The ROYAL CLIPPER at sea with a gentle following breeze.

The ROYAL CLIPPER'S bowsprit and figurehead.

The launch gets you to the beaches and small islands of the Caribbean.

On a photo expedition with the STAR FLYER in the Andaman Sea.

The STAR CLIPPER cruising off Valley Church beach, Antigua.

The STAR CLIPPER in the Classic Yacht Regatta of Antigua.

The Anda

The STAR FLYER under full canvas – a handsome subject for a photograph off the picturesque limestone cliffs of the Ko Hong Islands. The big sailing-ship glides without difficulty through the calm waters of the world-famous Phang Nga Bay; she only draws 6 metres (18 ft).

man Sea

Ko Miang, Ko Similan, Langkawi – the very names of the islands off Thailand and Malaysia promise the mysterious enchantment of exotic worlds. Strange-looking rock formations rear up from the glassy, intensely-hued waters of the Andaman Sea. The Star Flyer glides soundlessly through the delightful seascape, the dream of every adventurous traveller. The sailing-ship drops anchor in sleepy coves or bustling fishing-ports. Those who prefer to stay on board the Star Flyer feel like the captain in Joseph Conrad's story, *The Shadow-Line,* when he first takes command of his ship: »The shore to which she was moored was as if it did not exist. What were to me all the countries of the globe? In all the parts of the world washed by navigable waters our relation to each other would be the same – and more intimate than there are words to express in the language. Apart from that, every scene and episode would be a mere passing show.«

From Ko Hong to the coastline of Krabi. An expedition with the launch and the Zodiac inflatable, to take some photographs. The main subject of the outing is of course the STAR FLYER – a beautiful sight under full sail. Massive limestone cliffs and caves with weird stalactites hanging down form a strange and unreal backdrop. ➢ Over 120 of these unusual islets and forest-covered limestone peaks, rising rise high above the sea, belong to the 155 square-mile Phang Nga National Park. The power-boat heads for Ko Ping Gan, better know as the »James Bond island«.

2000

Dense rain-forest, rich in flora and fauna, covers the larger islands around Phuket in Thailand, as far south as Langkawi, off the west coast of Malaysia. The programme includes short trips into the jungle and a visit to a butterfly-farm. In Phuket, the exotic gardens of the Marina Cottage Hotel offer a botanical stroll.

Around the nine uninhabited islands of Ko Similan, the great coral reefs and the luxuriant underwater world of the tropics are among the best diving-waters in the world. The passengers who want to dive can check their equipment in the pool on board. Then it's a jump into the crystal-clear waters, sun-warmed to over 80° Fahrenheit, to snorkel, swim, splash about or scuba-dive – feeling as much at home in the water as a fish. ➢ The STAR FLYER lies at anchor off Ko Similan.

First, switch your cabin-tag on the board from »In« to »Out«, then climb into the launch for an all-day excursion to the islands of Ko Similan. Exploring or just lazing on the Robinson Crusoe beach can be as much fun as a climbing-tour through the picturesque rock-formations. ➢ Still a few inches of water under the keel: a »wet« landing, when the launch is beached.

The Beach-Bar is the first thing to be brought ashore. The cook, the waiter and the maître de cuisine struggle through the surf with the requisites for a beach picnic. Since there are some non-swimmers among both passengers and crew, the »beach-boys«, young men from the sports team, offer them a helping hand.

115

Riggers, the crewmen who work with the ropes and sails, must have a head for heights. On the masts of the Star Flyer – the tallest is 63 metres (207 feet) high – Andrey from Russia regularly checks shackles and bolts, and replaces bulbs in the navigation-lights. The 73-man crew comprises 19 nationalities – the UN on board the STAR FLYER. »Mr T.« as Roland the engineer is nicknamed, comes from St Lucia in the British West Indies.

On the great sailing-ships of the Star Clipper fleet you are free to do almost anything. But there is a strict ban on smoking in the cabins, and you are in trouble if you miss the safety-practice with life-jackets. Captain Jürgen Müller-Cyran introduces himself and his crew to the new passengers; he encourages them to take part in the sailing and even to climb up to the crow's-nest. In the daily »Captain's story-time« there is no spinning of old sailors' yarns; instead, the captain gives a fascinating insight into the history of the great sailing-ships and talks about seamanship.

The Star Flyer has dropped anchor of the island of Ko Khai Nok. In the background is the nearby coastline of Phuket. From the white sandy beach of this resort island you can lovingly admire »your« ship with her elegant, sweeping clipper-ship lines and the filigree of masts and rigging. A spicy fragrance wafts over the beach. Fishermen and their families are grilling their fresh catch over an open fire and cooking delicious Thai specialities in a wok with ginger, cardamom, coriander, lemon-grass, chili and limes.

The STAR FLYER is on a treasure-hunt through the cultures of South-East Asia – along the coast of southern Thailand, down to Malaysia and through the Straits of Malacca, the busiest shipping route between the Indian Ocean and the Pacific. The excursions ashore by the »farangs«, as travellers are called in Thailand, take them through strange scents and sounds, to see temple-dancing and singing.

天賜財源庆丰収
在場作品由产

The Car

The ROYAL CLIPPER, Queen of the Seas, is a five-masted sailing-ship, fully square-rigged on all five masts. She is currently the biggest sailing-ship in the world. Her design was inspired by the legendary PREUSSEN, owned by the Laeisz P-Line of Hamburg. Built in 1902, she was rammed and then beached near Dover in 1910.

i b b e a n

In the intensely-felt words of the novelist and sea-captain, Joseph Conrad: »The sky was wonderfully clear and blue. The sea lay smooth, blue, transparent, glittering like a precious stone, spread far on all sides, from horizon to horizon, as if the whole earth were a jewel, a vast sapphire, a single gem polished into a planet. The contrast of colours is truly fascinating – the white sails and the constantly changing turquoise blue of the sea.« Past the tropical vistas of evergreen volcanic islands, the STAR CLIPPER and the majestic ROYAL CLIPPER glide through the breathtaking world of the Caribbean. A world of contrasts, a melting-pot of Indian, African and European cultures. The great sailing-ships anchor in remote, secluded bays, or off bustling ports that invite you to plunge into the rhythmic Caribbean lifestyle.

Landfall off Grenada. The foredeck, with its row of cleats and its running-gear, points towards the picturesque capital, St George's. The infectious rhythms of a steel band, the brightly painted houses and a glass of rum punch all add to that Caribbean holiday mood. ➢ From the hillside of the exclusive Anse Chastanet hotel complex on St Lucia, you can look far out across the Soufriere Bay to the horizon. In a stopover on the trip, the Royal Clipper anchors off the striking landmark of the bay, the twin volcanic peaks known as the Pitons.

For the Royal Clipper, getting out of the 100-yard-wide Marigot Bay is a tricky manoeuvre. Captain Uli Pruesse has painted a chart of the harbour on to his hand, so that he has the narrow, 30-yard-wide channels and the safe distances from the reefs, right in front of his eyes. ➢ The Royal Clipper on the horizon, off the scenic Bottom Bay, Barbados.

Carried by the trade-winds through the Caribbean; from Bridgetown, Barbados, to the islands and beaches of the central and southern Caribbean. *Left-hand page, above:* anchoring off Saba; *centre:* alongside in the harbour of Fort de France in Martinique, and lying in the roadstead off St Barts and St Maarten; bottom: taking the launch to bathe and picnic on the uninhabited Grenadine cays. *Above:* Caribbean impressions.

Bequia is the northernmost of the Grenadine islands. The bay outside the sleepy »capital« of Port Elizabeth is a favourite rendezvous for yachtsmen. The waterfront is lined with cosy rum- and beer-bars. The yard-arms and masts of the ROYAL CLIPPER rise majestically skywards. Another five-masted ship, the WIND SURF, is no competition under sail. Beside the Queen of the Sea, she is like lumpfish-roe compared to caviar.

At anchor in a sheltered bay, the captain opens out the ROYAL CLIPPER'S marina platform. From there, getting in or on to the clear 80° water is easy and straightforward; then you can snorkel, dive or sail. ➢ »I never believed it could be so wonderful. The sight of those gigantic towers of canvas is to me more tremendous than the nave of a cathedral. It is so stately. The feeling of that gentle but irresistible force carrying us along – it's like floating on air,« wrote the author H. Hauser after his voyage on the four-masted barque PAMIR.

Imposing as the ships of the STAR CLIPPER fleet look from the outside, no less impressive is the sight that greets you on board – especially on the ROYAL CLIPPER. The glass bottom of her swimming pool forms part of the deck of a 3-storey atrium; it concentrates the sunlight and illuminates the murals and the restaurant. Portholes below the waterline give views into and out of Captain Nemo's Lounge, as well as the fitness and beauty centre. On all ships, the cabins and staterooms are tidied and cleaned twice a day.

Early morning on the ROYAL CLIPPER'S big sun-deck. Part of the daily ritual is hoisting the Clipper Line's house-flag. The masts are reflected in the freshly polished magnetic compass, but the gleaming belaying-pin made of stainless steel needs no such care. It is the modern replacement for a traditional fitting that was lathe-turned from wood.

Saturn B Mk2
STAR CLIPPERS

Having sailed in all the world's oceans, marine professionals like Captain Jürgen Müller-Cyran *(above left)* pass on their valuable knowledge and experience to the next generation. The newly appointed captain, Sergei Utitsin *(left-hand page)*, commands a crew of nearly 70 men and women from 20 nations. The working language on and off duty is English. The only exception is »Polly Parrot«, who is looked after in Russian by Oleg the rigger *(above centre)*.

Classic Ya

»Sheets hard in, we're going for the line!« at the start of the Tall Ship World Peace Cup of English Harbour, Antigua. »All hands on deck and to your stations!« The sails are set and constantly trimmed – over 3,300 square metres of canvas billow out against the blue sky.

cht Regatta

Crewing on a tall ship, a windjammer, in a regatta, is a magnificent experience, which was originally reserved only for professional sailors and sea-cadets. On board the four-masted barquentine STAR CLIPPER the passengers have the chance to help tend the ropes when beating to windward. »Let's get under way – all hands on deck. Hoist the sails, aft the braces!« Under the command of Captain Uli Pruesse everyone, from seven to seventy years old, is introduced to sailing and seamanship – the traditional hands-on kind, which brings romance to your heart. As the English poet John Masefield wrote: »I must go down to the seas again, to the lonely sea and the sky, And all I ask is a tall ship and a star to steer her by And the wheel's kick and the wind's song and the white sail's shaking, And a grey mist on the sea's face, and a grey dawn breaking.«

A hundred hands obey the captain's order. Uli Pruesse learned his skills on the foredeck, And has a gift for inspiring people with a love of sailing. Even confirmed landlubbers are fascinated to learn the most complicated wrinkles of traditional seamanship. His motto is: »Hands on is more fun!«

TALL SHIPS
WORLD PEACE CUP
ANTIGUA

The »shantymaster«, a man named Csaba, sets the rhythm in a »haul-shanty« for hoisting the sails, and everyone has to put their back into it: »Whisky calms the seaman's fears, whisky, Johnny! Me, I just say ›skol‹ and ›cheers‹, whisky for my Johnny!« Then the great moment comes, the ship gathers speed! Captain Uli Pruesse gives a cheer and shouts: »Now she's sailing!«. ➢ And the clipper slices through the waves.

Sea-dogs like the »Professor of Sailing«, James Dean, assist the captain in the induction and training of his eager students. Among the passengers, from retired admirals to grannies with their grandsons, many are sailing-freaks, and those who aren't now, certainly will be by the end of the trip. With the sails perfectly trimmed for a wind abeam, the STAR CLIPPER surges past the schooner Westward and up to the finishing-line. ➢ Everyone to their stations! The wind-god blows fit to crack his cheeks, and with sails reefed in a 25- to 30-knot trade-wind, the STAR CLIPPER reaches a speed of 15 knots.

STAR CLIPPERS

The Star Clipper, close hauled, ploughs an elegant course through a moderate sea. Because the ship heels in a stable way, due to the steady wind-pressure on the sails, she rises and falls in the water but does not roll from side to side as a steamship does. After three hours of racing, the finishing-line and the well-earned »sun-downer« are in sight. »Aft the mizzen-sheet!« Just as in the old windjammer days, the order is passed down the line.

The Medit

The Star Clipper speeds through the waves. What a sight! It seems like the rebirth of a bygone age – the age of navigation under sail, which lasted for 5,000 years. If this does not gladden your heart, then you don't have one – at least not for sailing.

e r r a n e a n

»But I have seen/pointing her shapely shadows from the dawn/an image tumbled on a rose-swept bay,/a drowsy ship of some yet older day.« So wrote the poet James Elroy Flecker in his Mediterranean elegy, *The Old Ships*. Sailing under splendid canvas, in the wake of the Phoenicians, Greeks and Romans, the Crusaders and the Venetians, is the best way to experience the mythology of the Aegean, the cradle of western civilisation, or the Balearic Islands, or the coasts of the Tyrrhenian Sea. This dream comes true on the Mediterranean cruises of the Star Clipper's wind-jammer fleet. Gnarled olive-trees overhang weather-worn tombs and ruins that bear witness to wars and campaigns of conquest. The lure of the azure-blue sea gives way to fascinating views of the land, revealing the romantic en-chantment of old churches and fortifications.

The STAR FLYER anchored off the old crusader castle on Rhodes. From the historic harbour it is only a few minutes walk to the fortified Old Town and its bazaar. In the evening the great sailing-ship glitters with festive illumination and Greek folklore is provided at the Tropical Bar. The pianist plays a song called »Greek Wine«, but the cocktail of the day has the un-Greek name of Mai Tai.

In a light breeze the sails are set and the yards braced; then on arrival the sails are furled. It requires a balancing-act in the bowsprit net to gather the foresails, which are fastened to the bowsprit with strops. This is part of the seaman's daily round, and it entertains the passengers on the clipper-ships. Those who are not happy just watching, can try their hand themselves. ➢ A stiff breeze in the Aegean.

The STAR FLYER sails into the amphitheatre created by a seismic upheaval – the crater of Santorini. Around 1500 B.C. the most violent volcanic eruption in ancient times hurled the island into the air. Perched nearly 1,000 feet above the harbour is the town of Thira, from where you can look down into the chasm of the extinct volcano. A highlight of any trip through the Cyclades.

From Piraeus, the port of Athens, the Aegean cruise continues along the coast of the Greek mainland, to the Temple of Poseidon on Cape Sounion. Then the beaches on the island of Mykonos and on to the little Turkish town of Bodrum. Right behind the fortress by the harbour is a vast market quarter. The last launch back to the ship leaves at 6 p.m. All aboard! The STAR FLYER sets course for the island of Hydra.

Dropping anchor off Hydra, the seafarers' island that achieved fame at the time of the Greek War of Liberation. On the island, with its unusual architecture and unspoilt charm, there are no cars rushing around, only donkeys and mules. Enjoying ouzo, fish and wine in a taverna, you can soak up the unique atmosphere of this Greek island and the idyllic view of the elegant STAR FLYER.

For Aeolus, god of the winds, sails are always easy prey, and the sailmaker's work is never done. It is no different on board a neighbouring ship, the legendary four-masted barque SEA CLOUD. »Everything ship-shape – all hands to cleaning« comes the order after a trip and re-provisioning. The »Tropical Deck« is scrubbed with soda-bleach and water. This not only makes it look smart, but also seals the planks.

Everyone on board has a set task and has to work in seamanly collaboration with his »mucker«, his shipmate. To maintain a perfect appearance, the ships are constantly scrubbed and polished, right down to the anchor. Women are, of course, not there simply as decorative figureheads but as full members of the crew. Gone are the old seafaring days when the saying was: »If they can't piss over the gunwale, they shouldn't be aboard!«

Early in the morning the ROYAL CLIPPER glides picturesquely under sail, but assisted by her 5,000 h.p. diesel engine, into the harbour of Port Hercule. For a day she lies as a floating hotel in one of the world's most sophisticated ports, at the foot of the grandest quarter and the many fine sights of the glittering Principality of Monaco. The sailing-ship has pride of place at the pier of Monte Carlo's yacht-harbour.

The Royal Clipper docks alongside in the idyllic harbour of Mahón on the Spanish Balearic island of Menorca, right in the »front parlour« of the town. The next morning, under full sail, she will pay a call on the larger sister-island of Mallorca, with its handsome cathedral. The little port of Palamos on the Costa Brava provides a berth for half a day. At 3 p.m., to the rousing strains of a farewell melody, Conquest of Paradise, the clipper sets sail and heads out to sea …

➢ Sail away …

Sail away

Who hath desired the sea? –
the immense and contemptuous surges?
The shudder, the stumble, the swerve, as the
star-stabbing bowsprit emerges?
The orderly clouds of the Trades, and the ridged,
roaring sapphire thereunder –
Unheralded cliff-haunting squalls and the
headsail's low-volleying thunder –

FROM *THE SEA AND THE HILLS* BY RUDYARD KIPLING

QUEEN OF THE SEAS

Anyone who clambers up to the crow's-nest on the mast of the ROYAL CLIPPER at sea, feels like an explorer in the brilliant morning sunshine. There is no engine vibration, no hum from propeller-shaft or thump from cylinders, no sooty plume from a funnel to destroy the illusion of witnessing the world being created afresh each day. The gently murmuring wind strokes the sails and sets the shrouds humming. It seems hoarse from roaring in the treacherous straits between Maddalena and Corsica; then it holds its breath along the Costa Smeralda, as though it had only been joking before. As far as the eye can see, there is not a tanker, a ferry, nor a container-ship – none of those normally ubiquitous merchant vessels that turn the boundless deep blue ocean into an asphalt-grey highway, fenced in by time and economics.

I had arranged for the sports-team from the ROYAL CLIPPER to take me in the fast red Zodiac inflatable and put me ashore on a jetty in the shimmering heat of Bonifacio, at the southern tip of Corsica, because I wanted to enjoy a landward view of the ship sailing into the narrows. The steep cliffs of pale grey granite, looming ever closer together, form a kind of small Mediterranean fjord, at the end of which a narrow harbour awaits incoming ships. It was there that I stood waiting for the big moment. For a long time nothing happened, except for the nimble water-taxis putt-putting out of the harbour, taking tourists to see the impressive caves beneath the cliff-perched Old Town. But suddenly there was a commotion among the tourists, who thanks to their better angle of vision, could see further out into the bay than I could. With a simultaneous movement, they all aimed their digital camcorders in the same direction. And then I too saw her rounding a rocky bluff: the ROYAL CLIPPER gliding into harbour under sail – like some unreal, dreamlike phantom from a long-gone era of maritime history.

Her arrival is like a queen making her entrance, too confident of her impact to wish to demand attention. There is no need for any hooting on the ship's klaxon, nor for any spectacular manoeuvring. I watch excitedly as Captain Uli Pruesse brings her majestically up to the quay and makes fast. As if rolled up by ghostly hands, the sails disappear on to the yards, giving a clear view of the criss-crossing shrouds and stays, braces and backstays. One might say the queen has taken her seat and removed her robe. Suddenly the harbour appears far too small, far too humdrum, and I am forcibly reminded of those familiar scenes where the Queen, visiting some randomly selected subjects, is shown into their modest terraced houses.

Everyone hurries to the quayside to look at the ship close to. Most people photograph whatever their pixels reveal, a number rely on the evidence of their own eyes, but nowhere did I spot that mixture of sour envy and secret admiration that frequently haunts the faces of those strolling round the yacht-marinas in Monte Carlo or Puerto Banus. This ship is plainly not the toy of some plutocrat or aristocrat. There are no guards or barriers to keep the public at a safe distance. No limousines roll up to the gangway. The people coming ashore in their holiday clothes are just like you and me, people who can afford to put into practice the notion that getting somewhere is not the object, but that what matters is *how* you get there. The atmosphere on

Captain's story-time« with skipper Jürgen Müller-Cyran on the sun-deck, with exciting tales and practical hints on navigation. He has spent half his life at sea, and real life for him is everything to do with ships and the sea. If specially requested, the skipper will conduct marriage ceremonies – albeit not legally binding ones.

the quayside is a relaxed blend of amazement and delight. And then, after sundown, as the ROYAL CLIPPER lies majestically, illuminated to her topmasts with little glowing bulbs, she adds her cloak of lights to the glittering confusion of the cosmos, as though she were simply another galaxy.

Wherever we sailed with the ROYAL CLIPPER in the days that followed – to Porto Cervo in Sardinia, Porto Ferraio in Elba, or the bay of Portovenere, which has been known as the *Golfo dei Poeti*, ever since Lord Byron lived there and his friend Percy Bysshe Shelley capsized in a boat and drowned – everywhere the ship was greeted like a monarch graciously granting an audience. In some places she lay at a discreet distance in the roadstead, and dispatched her tenders as vassals, elsewhere she squeezed herself into the harbour, as if into a dress that is too tight.

Romantic embellishment? Of course. But that's exactly why the ROYAL CLIPPER was built. It is the declared purpose of the Swedish ship-owner Mikael Krafft to enable his guests on the three sailing-ships of his Star Clipper Line – which includes the STAR FLYER and the STAR CLIPPER as well as the ROYAL CLIPPER – to experience the beauty of traditional sailing, combined with all the benefits of today's luxury. And needless to say, the safety of high-tech seamanship comes guaranteed. For fascinating as it may be to make an astral observation with the aid of a sextant – especially when someone as entertaining as Captain Uli Pruesse explains it to his passengers – the actual fixing of the ship's position has for years now been carried out by the GPS system, which technology-obsessed motorists will know from their in-car direction-finding programmes. Thanks to data transmitted round the clock by the Globus geostationary satellites, your current location can be established to within half a metre. By now this system is so commonplace that quite a number of passengers carry it around in a wristwatch-sized format and officiously check the helmsman's accuracy.

But if you look on board for the traditional radio-room with Morse-code telegraph and radio operators wearing rubber-lined headphones, you will not find them. Dedication to tradition certainly does not mean ignoring technical advances. Today, like other ships, the STAR CLIPPERS receive wind and weather warnings as well as SOS messages and information about collisions and shipwrecks, all through what is known as NAVTEX – printed

data transmitted by radio. Moreover, in an emergency at sea, assistance can be called up anywhere in the world with the satellite-based Global Maritime Distress and Safety System (GMDSS). All the lifeboats in the Clipper fleet are also equipped with this system. When safety is at stake, there is no room for starry-eyed romanticism, and for this reason all Clipper ships, needless to say, have the benefit of weather-radar and echo-sounders, smoke-sensors and sprinklers, and thus meet the requirements of Lloyds highest safety rating – 100A1. The sensation of crossing the oceans just as men did in the great days of sail, should not be accompanied by the dangers to which seamen were then exposed.

That is why all three ships are equipped with very powerful marine engines – the STAR FLYER and STAR CLIPPER each have a 1,360 h.p. Caterpillar diesel, and the ROYAL CLIPPER two engines with a total output of 5,000 h.p. – not the least of whose tasks is to make sure the cruise schedule can be maintained even with contrary winds or a flat calm. The motto is: sail as often as possible; use power only when necessary. Anyone who has read Joseph Conrad's vivid description of a »dead calm« in the dreaded doldrums around the equator, which could last several weeks and drove many a seaman to madness, will be grateful for the convenience of this combination of wind and motor power.

The sunlight falls on the glass floor of the swimming-pool, producing dramatic reflections in the atrium, which descends through three deck-levels – from the sun-deck to the piano bar, and down to the restaurant. The ROYAL CLIPPER'S opulent décor has been created by top American architect Donald Starkey, and the fantasist murals are the work of the German artist Rainer Maria Latzke.

Ships' figureheads have always had a number of functions: some were decoration and adornment, others served to ward off enemies or to give protection against the spirits of storm and sea. Marie Krafft, the daughter of the ship-owner, modelled for the ROYAL CLIPPER'S figurehead, which was sculpted by Birgit and Klaus Hartmann. The STAR FLYER is adorned with a gilded sea-eagle.

To avoid too great a sacrifice of passenger comfort, even in high winds, the ROYAL CLIPPER has also been fitted with stabilisation-tanks, in which up to 160 tons of water can be pumped through a network of pipes to the windward side, in order to flatten the angle of heel, in other words to minimise the tilt of the ship.

Much as the Star Clippers may outwardly resemble the windjammers on which they have been modelled, they really have little in common with them. The great sailing-ships, whose heyday lasted from the mid-19th century to the end of the First World War, were combined cargo and passenger vessels. It is true that they offered a few far-from-luxurious cabins, but the bulk of the passengers were housed in tiny bunks, or even more uncomfortably, in vast sleeping-saloons on evil-smelling passenger decks. The main diet was dried fish, relieved twice a week by salted meat and tinned vegetables. Some ships carried live pigs on board, which were slaughtered during the voyage. There was no electricity on those ships, so there was no chance of keeping fresh food in freezers or ice-machines. Drinking-water, carried in large tanks, was a precious commodity. The very thought of such conditions makes today's »gastronauts« shudder as they feast from

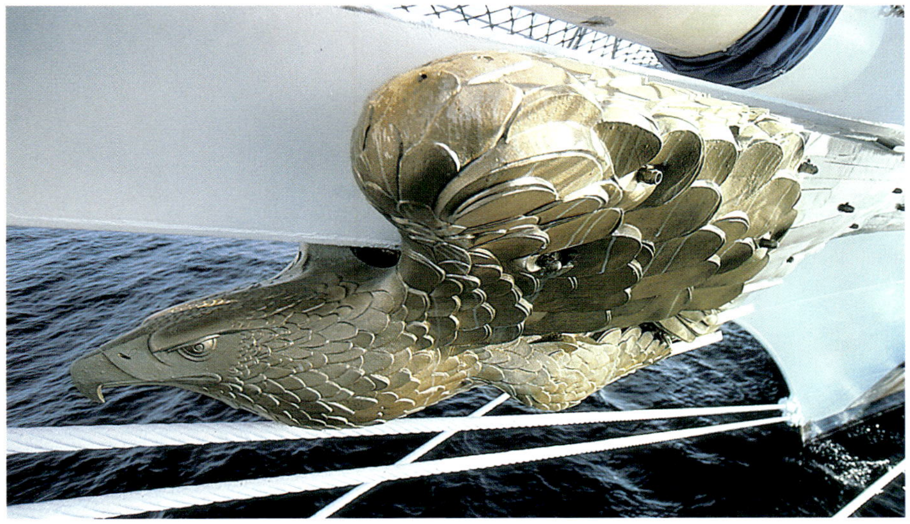

the buffets laden with fresh fish, meat, fruit and vegetables of every kind, and wines from the world's finest vineyards.

Looked at in more detail, the three vessels of Star Clippers Inc. are based on two different types of ship, a fact which becomes clear from the pattern of their sails and rigging. The STAR FLYER and STAR CLIPPER, both designed by the Englishman Robert MacFarlane (hull) and the Dutchman Olivier van der Meer (rigging), are classic clippers known as four-masted barquentines; the ROYAL CLIPPER, on the other hand, is fast five-master. She measures 134 metres (440 feet) over all, is a fully square-rigged ship and is built for luxury cruising throughout the world. She is modelled on the famous five-masted square-rigger PREUSSEN, built with the strength to round Cape Horn, though that cargo sailing-ship had an overall length of 147 metres (482 feet). The ROYAL CLIPPER is thus descended from the windjammers. Incidentally, the word has nothing to do with the German word *jammern*, »to wail«, though when becalmed you could be sure to hear at least one sailor moaning on the deck of such a ship. It is in fact derived from the English verb »to jam«, in the sense of »press« or »squeeze«, and expresses the notion of a fully laden ship with sails trimmed for maximum speed, sailing hard on the wind and squeezing every last ounce of energy from it.

Why is it that in the last few decades these clippers have experienced such an impressive renaissance in the cruise sector of tourism? It is because they represent perfection in the art and skill of the shipbuilder. They combine the aesthetic fascination of elegant lines with high dynamic efficiency, they demand top performance from their crew and in return give the highest degree of satisfaction to the keen sailor. On board these ships, what still counts is a feeling for the tides, for interaction with nature and for the struggle with primeval forces. They are both traditional and modern – quite simply the ultimate dream-ships.

The FLYING CLOUD, launched in 1851 from Donald McKay's shipyard in Boston, was the fastest clipper of her day. She could reach 15 knots and in 1851 set a speed record of 89 days and 8 hours for the voyage from San Francisco to New York via Cape Horn.

GREYHOUNDS OF THE SEA

But in a gale, the silent machinery of a sailing-ship would catch not only the power, but the wild and exulting voice of the world's soul.

JOSEPH CONRAD, FROM *THE MIRROR OF THE SEA*

Since time immemorial, two parameters have determined the value of a ship: its cargo capacity and its speed, and these two measures are closely related to each other. The higher the cargo tonnage was, the lower would be the speed, though of course hull-shape and sail-area were contributing factors. The clippers built from the mid-19th century onwards had significantly smaller cargo capacity compared to other types of vessel, but could sail faster than any rivals at the time. Essentially, three factors contributed to their development: with the disappearance of Britain's East India Company, which ceased trading in 1831, speed became an important criterion for merchant shipping. Up to that point, speed had been of little importance, since in 1600 the company had been granted a trading monopoly by Queen Elizabeth I. The typical fat-bellied galleons of those days could wait at their leisure for favourable winds for the voyages to and from India, particularly since with their square-rigged sails they could sail no closer than 60 degrees to the wind. It was not unusual for voyages in these ships, to the East Indies or Australia, whose coast James Cook had explored in 1771, to last for five or six months.

It was in fact the carrying of human cargo that demanded ever faster ships. The plight of the lower classes and the harsh penalties for crime in the second half of the 18th century had filled Britain's prisons to bursting-point. The government could only see one solution: the delinquents would have to be deported to faraway Australia, to the place where Captain Cook had first landed, Botany Bay, not far from the great natural harbour that is today called Sydney. Journey-time now became a crucial factor, since the convict passengers naturally had to be fed during the voyage, and that pushed up the costs, even though the prisoners were fobbed off with the plainest and cheapest of sustenance. From 1788, when captain Arthur Phillip brought his first human cargo to the new colony of New South Wales on Australia's east coast, until 1840 when the transportation of convicts was brought to an end, Britain used sea-routes to colonise the new continent inland from the east coast and later, with voluntary settlers, from the west coast as well.

Pressure for more speed also came, needless to say, from the slave trade. In ships just 30 metres (100 feet) long, as many as 600 black Africans – mostly from what are now Senegal and the Congo – were crammed together and chained in tight rows on the lower decks. The men and women had either been captured or else sold by their tribal

The Cruise Director, in this case Peter Kissner, is the most important man on the ship, after the captain. He attends to the wellbeing of the guests on board as well as on excursions ashore, and arranges the daily entertainment. At each port of call he supplies information about the country and its people, about the procedure for getting in and out of the launches and the importance of maintaining a sure grip at all times.

chiefs to slave-hunters, and on average 15 per cent of them died during the arduous Atlantic crossing from the west coast of Africa to the slave-markets of the Caribbean and the Americas. The sanitary conditions on board were indescribable; food and water were kept to a minimum. The longer a voyage lasted, the greater was the risk of sickness, epidemic or revolt.

The third thing that favoured the development of swifter ships, of which clippers can be seen as the culmination, was the notorious opium trade between India and China. Since vessels that wanted to have a share in this hugely lucrative business, had to be capable of making the eastward voyage from India to China against the westerly monsoon, it was the American ships, with their combination of square- and fore-and-aft rig, that had a great advantage over the frigates preferred by European ship-owners. The clippers carried opium from Bengal to southern China where, together with silver, it was accepted in exchange for tea and silk. The first ship to arrive in a European or American port laden with treasures from China, naturally got the best prices for them. The profits were often so high that the construction of a new clipper could be financed from them.

In 1848, gold was discovered in California, and two years later in Australia. Both places were stormed by hordes of gold-prospectors, fortune-hunters and adventurers lured by the promise of instant wealth. Australia could only be reached by sea in any case, but most of California's »forty-niners« also chose the sea-route, since crossing the American continent overland was generally considered too exhausting and dangerous. With the gold-rush, the heyday of the clippers began, for now time really was money. This was the age of the Cape Horners. There was no Panama Canal then, and to travel by sea from the east to the west coast of the United States, it was necessary to round the southernmost tip of the American continent – Cape Horn – through waters feared by seamen, on account of the many small, rock-girt islands, the unpredictable winds and adverse currents. The cape had been discovered as long ago as 1616 by the Dutchman C. van Schouten who, with Isaac Le Maire, had led an expedition from Amsterdam along the east coast of America. Like many before and after them, they were searching for that elusive Terra Australis Incognita, a mysterious continent whose existence was necessary, so scientists of the day had calculated mathematically, on the grounds that

the stable rotation of the earth required the weight of the northern and southern hemispheres to be equal. Yet all that van Schouten and Le Maire had found, between the mainland of Tierra del Fuego and Staten Island to the south-east (now Argentina's Isla de los Estados), was a group of small offshore islands, the southernmost tip of which they named »Kap Hoorn«, after Schout's home town of Hoorn in Holland.

In the age of exploration, it was customary to name geographical features in this way. It was considered to be a verbal claim, often followed by physical occupation. But that was not the only reason. Particular landmarks such as mountains, bays or promontories were only ever discovered from the sea. They had to be indicated immediately on charts and maps, and therefore needed names. It was simply not possible to take over the names or descriptions given them by their aboriginal inhabitants.

The rounding of the dreaded Cape Horn used to be measured in the number of days a ship took to sail from latitude 50° S., southward round the cape, then along the west coast of Tierra del Fuego (now part of Chile) and northward back across latitude 50°. If winds and currents were particularly unfavourable, this took months. The German square-rigger SUSANNA set a depressing record with a passage lasting 99 days. Yet in 1938 the four-masted barque PRIWALL covered the same stretch in just six days. This gives a dramatic indication of how defenceless both a ship and her crew were against the forces of nature.

Because of their slender lines the clippers were not really suitable as pure cargo carriers, but instead as packet- and passenger-vessels. Thanks to their ability to sail close hauled to the wind, they were considered ideal Cape Horners. The typical route of an American clipper in the mid-19th century began on the eastern seaboard of the United States, then south to Tierra del Fuego, round Cape Horn, and northward up the coasts of South and Central America and as far as San Francisco. There it often happened that the crew were lured ashore by gold, so that the captain had no choice but to hire new crewmen with little inexperience or dubious moral character and continue the voyage across the Pacific to China, where the ship was loaded with tea and silk. In those days the London market paid twice as much for the first shipment of tea as for the second. Thus speed triumphed over cargo capacity. As soon

It is not just in the luxury cabins and staterooms of the STAR CLIPPER fleet that the mahogany panelling gleams and highly polished brass lamps and fittings add their lustre. All the ship's accommodation is equipped with the classic features of a private yacht, in a style true to the old seafaring tradition.

as the tea was unloaded, European emigrants were embarked for the USA. Versatility was the clipper's unbeatable advantage. Within a short time the round trip, New York – San Francisco – China – Europe – New York, was so profitable that the demand for clippers rose by leaps and bounds. In those days the shipyards in and around Boston alone employed 10,000 men. Whereas in 1850 precisely 16 clippers were built in American yards, two years later the figure had risen to 61, and in 1853 to an impressive 125.

One of the most successful and innovative designers in this shipbuilding boom was Donald McKay, born in Nova Scotia in 1810. It was his yard in East Boston that launched the first clipper, the STAG HOUND, in 1850. At the time it was reckoned to be the largest merchant-ship in the world. With her first voyage, from New York to Honk Kong via San Francisco, its owners, two Boston merchants, had already made enough to recoup her building costs. Three years later McKay built the GREAT REPUBLIC, a four-masted barque, and the largest wooden ship ever to sail the oceans. With her length of 102 metres (335 feet) and a massive total sail-area of 13,000 square metres, McKay thought she would be the pride of his clipper fleet. But in the construction of ships entirely from wood, the maximum length was the »magic« figure of 65 metres (213 feet), beyond which the necessary rigidity could no longer be guaranteed. To overcome this limitation, McKay used metal components for the first time to connect the different sections of the hull – and so the use of wood and metal in combination, the composite construction method that was later to become common, was born.

However, even before her maiden voyage, the GREAT REPUBLIC caught fire in New York harbour; admittedly she was saved, but it was several years before she went into service, and then it was with a reduced rig and lower tonnage. Sailors, always superstitious, believed the ship was cursed and shunned her, even though she proved her worth by covering the distance from New York to Liverpool in 13 days. In 1869, the GREAT REPUBLIC was sold to the Merchant Trading Company of Liverpool, and under the name DENMARK she was employed mainly in the East Indies trade. Three years later, bound for Rio de Janeiro, she was caught in a hurricane off Bermuda, sprang a leak and had to be abandoned. The curse had taken its toll.

None other of the more than fifty other ships that McKay built, met such a sad fate. The fact that this befell his showpiece clipper was an especially bitter blow for him.

On each ship in the STAR CLIPPER fleet there is a comfortable, wood-panelled library with a wrought-iron fireplace. The Edwardian-styled interior décor on the ROYAL CLIPPER and the antique ship paintings are a reminder of the great age of sail.

Among his other ships, the clipper FLYING CLOUD stands out. In 1851 she completed the New York – San Francisco trip in 89 days, faster than any sailing-ship of her class had ever done it. During the voyage she reached a maximum speed of 18 knots and in one 24-hour period, covered the astonishing distance of 374 nautical miles. In the years that followed the clippers competed under racing conditions but failed to beat this record performance. McKay's designs had proved themselves the fastest and most streamlined.

So it is not surprising that the Swedish shipowner Mikael Krafft went back to McKay's drawings when, in the 1990s, he realised his childhood dream by building the STAR FLYER and the STAR CLIPPER, and in so doing revived the fascinating age of the clipper-ships in order to bring it closer to a public of traditionally minded sailing enthusiasts. The ships would not be mere carbon-copies of the old clippers, but new designs based on McKay's brilliant lines, and incorporating the latest developments in their rig and fitting out. Krafft opted to rig both ships as four-masted barquentines. This means that while the foremast is square rigged, the remaining three masts carry a fore-and-aft schooner rig, with four staysails, three jibs, a mizzen and two of the famous »fisherman« sails. It is therefore possible, without the square-sails and with only the schooner-sails, to sail closer to the wind than other square-rigged ships. The square-sails can be rolled up on to the yard-arms hydraulically from deck level, in a horizontal version of the familiar roller-jib, developed by Krafft himself. All the other sails can also be set, trimmed or furled from the deck, so that the ship can be sailed with a deck-crew of five, whereas the old clippers needed as many as ten times that number of deckhands, depending on their design.

The journals of James Cook and other great seafarers suggest that voyages of discovery were also to some extent voyages of *self*-discovery. It is from this that the myth of the man who has to prove himself at sea, draws its power and fascination. From Homer's *Odyssey* to Joseph Conrad's *Lord Jim*, it has been a recurring motif in European art and literature. Sailing combines within itself the two opposing principle in daring human endeavour: danger and cunning. We can move in an element that proverbially offers no support, with the aid of another element that we can neither see nor grasp. Nothing is more elusive than a puff of wind, nothing more destructive than a hurricane. This alternation between being at the mercy of the elements and attempting to become

their master is a common metaphor for our path through life. That is why many sailors' sayings have found their way into our language: »casting oil on troubled waters«, »getting one's bearings«, being »adrift« or »stranded«, giving someone »a fair wind« or liking »the cut of his jib«, being »blown off course« or having »a steady hand at the helm«. The examples are endless.

The clippers vanished as swiftly as they had appeared. Along with various economic and political factors, it was principally the construction of two canals that literally took the wind from the sails of these trading vessels. In 1869 the Suez Canal was opened, cutting more than three and half thousand miles off the voyage to the East Indies, since ships no longer had sail round Africa and the Cape of Good Hope, but went directly from the Mediterranean to the Red Sea. Then the Panama Canal, opened in 1914, spelled the end for the windjammers. Up to that point, steamships with their slower – albeit steady and predictable – speed, and the fact that the vast amount of coal they needed took up valuable cargo space, were at a disadvantage compared to clippers over long voyages. But the advent of the Suez Canal made steamships much more attractive, and indeed for the first time they could now be used on the trade routes to China and the East Indies. Because the wind conditions in the Red Sea prevented the clippers from sailing there, and because they would anyway have to be towed the 120 miles through the Suez Canal, the sailing-ships continued to use the old route to China via the cape of Good Hope. This voyage took 110 to 120 days, while steamships covered the shorter distance through the Suez Canal in half that time. The rapid decline of the clippers on this route is illustrated by the fate of the CUTTY SARK. Built in the Scottish town of Dumbarton on the river Clyde, in the same year that the Suez Canal was opened, she was intended as a challenger to the THERMOPYLAE, then the fastest of the tea-clippers. Her name, which now graces a brand of whisky, and means »short shirt« in Scottish dialect, was taken from a poem by Robert Burns about a beautiful witch named Nannie, who was also represented by the figurehead. The ship was a composite construction of teak and steel components, had an overall length of 85 meters (279 feet) and could set more than 3,000 square metres of sail on her three masts. On her first trip in 1870, the CUTTY SARK was the »first ship home«, in other words the first to land her cargo of tea in London. However, the THERMOPYLAE

»Halyards clear to run on deck!« comes the order from the bridge, when the »fishermen«, the two largest sails on board the STAR CLIPPER and the STAR FLYER are set. They are chiefly used in light winds and have to be furled by hand. Patching the sails is also manual work.

had not taken part in the race. In the next two years the CUTTY SARK lost to her rival, and in 1876, after only seven years at sea, she made her last tea voyage. After an obscure interlude as a coal-carrier, she then spent several years bringing wool from Australia to Britain. In 1893 she actually won a race from England to Sydney against the British steamship BRITANNIA. Yet even on that route the manpower-intensive clippers soon lost out to the competition from steam. The CUTTY SARK, once the finest clipper of all time, was sold to a Portuguese ship-owner, who renamed her FERREIRA, and later LA PEQUENA CAMISOLA (»short shirt« in Portuguese), then sold her on.

Re-rigged as a two-masted brigantine in 1916, the now very run-down ship bore the name MARIA DI AMPARO. But a storm in the English Channel in 1922 proved to be her salvation. She was towed, severely damaged into the Cornish port of Falmouth, where she was spotted by Captain Wilfred Dowman, who had begun his career as a ship's boy on the CUTTY SARK. He bought the ship as she was about to be broken up, had her renovated and gave her back her original name. When Dowman died in 1936, the CUTTY SARK went through various incarnations, including that of a training-ship, until she came into the hands of the Cutty Sark Preservation Society. This charitable association lovingly restored the clipper to her original glory, and moved her to her final berth, beside the National Maritime Museum in Greenwich, on the Thames east of London, where she continues to be a popular tourist attraction.

THE LAST GIANTS

The sea knows no friendship. Its generosity is reserved for those who have the sense to plumb its secrets, the courage to sustain its blows, the will to withstand its harshness

E. Morrison

Yet the sailing-ships rose up once more against the stink and thump of their steam-powered competitors. The final chapter of those merchantmen of sail was written in the remote harbours of Chile and Australia. It was the chapter of the windjammers. Originally this word was a term of abuse used by British sailors to describe the gaff-rigged American schooners, which could sail closer to the wind than the square-riggers, and whose crews could handle the sails in comfort from the deck, instead of having to clamber up the rigging. When the heyday of sail in mercantile navigation was already over, the windjammers were described as those last giants, who attempted to hold their own against steam. Their load-bearing structure, as it were the skeleton of the ship, on to which wooden planks were fixed to form the outer hull, was made of steel, a material new to shipbuilding, which was employed for the first time in the construction of the Cutty Sark.

Ever since seafaring began, six thousand years earlier, ships had been built entirely of wood. As a raw material it was freely available, easy to work and it floated in water. To build ships from iron, which itself has no buoyancy, was at first inconceivable to many sailors. The principle of uplift through water displacement was purely a mathematical concept, the practical effect of which was at first doubted by many. Nevertheless, this method of construction, which began in Britain in the 1860s, soon spread throughout the world, with the exception of the United States, which had an inexhaustible supply of cheap timber in the forests of the eastern seaboard. But the advantages of steel were plain to see, especially in the rigging. Steel masts, being hollow, were much lighter than wooden ones, yet possessed significantly greater rigidity, which meant they could be taller and thus provided greater sail area; shrouds and stays made of steel wire could sustain higher tension and were less liable to chafing than their forerunners of hemp. The construction principle

The Preussen at her birthplace, the Tecklenborg yard at Geestemünde, near Bremen, where she was built under the direction of her designer, Georg W. Claussen, and launched in 1902. As the flagship of the Laeisz Line she was the epitome of sailing-ship construction in an age that was already turning increasingly away from large sailing vessels.

The crew of the five-masted square-rigger PREUSSEN. »Don't go to sea, son; it ain't no ball. The work's damned hard and the pay's too small. The Devil should be a seaman!« That was the warning of an old sailors' song. For despite technological advances, the work and conditions at sea were tough.

whereby vertical metal sheets are riveted to a horizontally strutted framework, made it possible to build ships of a length not thought possible before, and at the same time to improve rigidity. Technical innovations such as mechanical winches developed by the Scotsman, Captain J.C.Jarvis, reduced the cost of crewing the big new sailing-ships. Operations such as bracing the yard-arms, previously an exhausting task for at least ten men, could now be carried out by two men, with the aid of Jarvis's winches. In order to give mechanical assistance to particularly heavy winding-gear, such as the windlass for the anchor, or to the bilge-pumps, many windjammers had small steam-engines on board purely for that purpose. However, the ships themselves were driven by wind-power alone. With the lengthened hull and thus increased cargo capacity, there was a desire to gain more speed, and so the number of masts was increased. Originally, the most common type of windjammer had three masts, but in 1880 ships were built with four, and the year after that with five and six masts. The THOMAS W. LAWSON, launched in 1902, with a length of 123 metres (403 feet) had no less than seven masts and was to be the largest of all multi-mast sailing-ships. But with this vessel the limit of »big is beautiful« was reached. After one Atlantic crossing the THOMAS W. LAWSON sank ignominiously off the coast of England. From then on ship-owners settled for three, four or five masts.

The square-rigged windjammers were employed by choice on the long voyages from Europe to Australia and Chile. To Chile they carried coal and industrial goods, and they returned with guano, the natural fertiliser formed by the droppings of the native seabirds on the rocky islands off the coasts of Chile and Peru. In addition, they brought back saltpetre, a mineral used in the manufacture of nitrogen-based fertilisers and also of gunpowder. At the beginning of the 20th century this route still went round Cape Horn, and those who had overcome this hazard were proud to count themselves among the Cape Horners, a kind of chivalric order among seamen. For the dreaded headland exacted its tribute, both human and material, from the windjammers. In the years from 1900 to 1915 alone, fifty-three vessels foundered, often with all lives lost, on the storm-lashed rocks of that southernmost tip of the Americas. The last windjammer to be claimed by Cape Horn, on 25 April 1923, was the one-time German ship PINNAS, which later sailed under the Finnish flag of the notorious, cost-cutting ship-owner, Gustaf Erikson. Twenty-five miles south of Diego Ramirez she began taking water, then lost her masts in a storm and had to be abandoned. Rusting relics of these courageous, but so often tragically doomed struggles with the Cape can still be seen at Port Stanley, in the Falkland Islands.

The opening of the Panama Canal on 15 August 1914 virtually brought an end to passenger traffic on sailing-ships. But windjammers continued to ply the Cape Horn route to Chile, since they were still superior to the steamships of those days, both in speed and cargo capacity. Money was still to be made here, since of course saltpetre was in ever greater demand for agriculture, and even more so for Europe's rapidly arming military forces.

It was Carl Laeisz, heir to the shipping line founded by his father Ferdinand in 1878, who correctly foresaw this development and therefore commissioned the building of a series of windjammers. They were known admiringly as the »Flying P« liners, because the names of the black-painted ships all began with the letter P, something inspired by the nickname of the owner's wife – »Poodle«. Together with the sailing freighters of the French owner A.D.Bordes, they dominated the Europe – South America and Europe – Australia routes from the beginning of the 20th century up to the outbreak of the First World War. Laeisz commissioned windjammers such as the PAMIR, PASSAT, PINNAS and PEIHO, and placed them under the command of captains who ranked with the best in the world.

In 1902 the heavy-weather sailing-ship PREUSSEN was the only five-masted square-rigger in the world, and the pride of the Laeisz shipping line. »When she ploughed across the sparkling blue Atlantic in a trade-wind, beneath a cathedral of white sails, the PREUSSEN was not simply beautiful, not just an exhilarating vision of symmetry and seemingly weightless elegance, she was more, she had the majesty of a queen. Anyone who saw her, fell silent.«

JOCHEN BREMMECKE, A CAPE HORNER

The command of a »P« line vessel was one of the most coveted positions the shipping world had to offer. Skippers like Boye Petersen or Robert Hilgendorf, who was known as »The Hamburg Demon« and »The Flying German«, are legends. Laeisz himself supervised the assembling of the crews right down to the lowliest member. He let it be known that »ship's boys will only be taken on if personally approved by me; I will only accept the sons of seafarers, who have grown up by the water; the captain can recommend such young men to me.«

In 1900 Laeisz ordered a ship from the Johann C. Tecklenborg shipyard in Geestemünde. Named the PREUSSEN, she was to be the flagship of his fleet and to this day remains unique among all the great sailing-ships. At the suggestion of Robert Hilgendorf, the vessel was designed by Georg W. Claussen, a marine architect who had learned his craft in Scotland and was compared to the great Donald McKay of Boston. Until the building of the ROYAL CLIPPER, the PREUSSEN was the only five-masted sailing ship, that is to say the only one carrying cargo, on which all five masts were square-rigged. With a waterline length of 135.5 metres (147 metres, or 482 feet over all) and a beam of 16 metres (52 feet), the hull was plated with the newly developed »soft« steel from Siemens-Martin. The main-mast soared to a height of 57 metres (187 feet) above the deck and the five masts together carried up to 48 sails with a total area of 5,560 square metres. All the shrouds, as well as the 1,168 blocks on the running-gear, were made from galvanised steel. The PREUSSEN had five watertight bulkheads and a double-skinned bilge, also divided by bulkheads, which were intended to make her unsinkable. With a draft of slightly over 8 metres (26 feet), the PREUSSEN could carry 8,000 tons of cargo, equal to 18 freight-trains of 30 wagons each. The ship had her own steam-powered derricks, enabling her to be loaded in what was then the record time of one week. So she was a ship of superlatives, the epitome of a windjammer.

On 31 July 1902 the PREUSSEN sailed on her maiden voyage to the Chilean port of Inique, to pick up a cargo of saltpetre. It was a trip she made thirteen times in all. Under full sail she could achieve a maximum speed of 17 knots, and in the South Atlantic in 1903 she covered a distance of 368 nautical miles in 24 hours, at an average speed of 15.3 knots. Her fastest time from the English Channel to Chile was 53 days. These are remarkable achievements, and it is all too easy to forget what exhausting and dangerous physical work was demanded of the 48 seamen who sailed this ship.

The kind of thing that happened when the men on watch had to climb up to the yard-arms in a storm, is vividly described by the chronicler of the PREUSSEN, Horst Hamecher: »The guy-ropes and buntlines were manned, the boatswains and other experienced men stood ready on the sheets, and at the appropriate order, these were thrown free and the guy-ropes and buntlines simultaneously hauled in with all strength and speed. Once all the sails were brought up to their yard-arms, the men climbed aloft. This was always done on the windward side. In this way they were pushed against the shrouds by the wind. That gave them more safety than if they had climbed up on the lee side, where the wind would have pushed them off and into the sea. Slowly but surely they make the long climb up the rigging. The storm howled in their ears; the sails and ropes screamed in an infernal chorus. When they reached the yard-arms they leaned over them, while standing on the swaying foot-ropes, furled the sail and lashed it firmly to the yard. Here, too, they began on the windward side, since here the sail was most exposed to the wind's assault. It was a tough job! The stiff canvas, as hard as a board when wet, the powerful gale, the size and weight of the sail itself – all added up to really backbreaking work. And far below them, the boiling sea. The captain stood on deck with a megaphone, has words half blown away: »...not done yet?«

It is a cruel irony of fate that, of all things, it would be a small, slow steamship that put an end to the PREUSSEN'S respected reputation as »Queen of the Seas«. It happened in the English Channel on the night of 5 to 6 November 1910. The PREUSSEN was sailing down the Channel bound for Chile with a few passengers, and a cargo of pianos, since in those days it was preferable to transport those by sailing-ship rather than expose them to the constant juddering of a steamship's engines. She was making 4 knots in fog and on a relatively calm sea. The steamship BRIGHTON was approaching on a collision course. »Helm hard a-port and back the aft yards,« ordered the PREUSSEN'S captain, Hinrich Nissen, as soon as he saw the steamer. The BRIGHTON'S captain, Albert E. Hemmings, had completely miscalculated the speed of the PREUSSEN and thought he could cross her bows. When the vessels collided, the PREUSSEN'S bowsprit sliced the funnel off the BRIGHTON, which in turn tore some bow plates from the PREUSSEN'S hull. This left a gash nearly 14 feet long that extended below the waterline. Sea water rushed in and very quickly flooded the forepeak. Being fitted with watertight bulkheads, this was not in itself a problem for the PREUSSEN. Nissen ordered the pumps to be started and the sails furled; he intended to make for Portsmouth. But the wind freshened and put paid to his plan. The tug ALERT was summoned, but was too underpowered to pull the PREUSSEN, with no engines of her own, against the wind. So Nissen attempted to alter course for Dover and to stop on the way off the sandy promontory of Dungeness.

By now all the passengers were on deck, tensely observing operations. The wind had become stronger, so that when an attempt was made to anchor, the port and starboard chains roared out under immense strain and were lost. Nissen was unable to manoeuvre his stricken vessel in any sensible manner. The south-westerly wind rose to gale force. Three more tugs arrived and tried desperately to pull the unwieldy monster to the safety of Dover harbour. Then, as if a hidden hand were pursuing some evil design, a gust came up and swept the whole convoy towards the chalk cliffs of the South Foreland. Since all four ships were in great danger and the pilot was getting nervous, Nissen ordered all the warps to the tugs to be cut and tried his luck in a last desperate sailing manoeuvre; he set the lower main topsail and ordered the yards on the after masts to be braced aback. This was intended to swing the PREUSSEN away from the cliffs again. But at about 16.30 hours on 6 November the damaged bow section hit a submerged rock off the coast, the ship grounded and her groaning hull veered round parallel to the coast. The storm and heavy seas flung the defenceless ship on to the rocks and Nissen had to abandon her. The sails and cargo were saved. But the site of this shipwreck, Crab Bay near Dover, not only became the grave of the Queen of the Seas, it was also the writing on the wall for the windjammers in general.

The outbreak of the First World War in 1914 dealt a heavy blow to European sailing freighters. German U-boats alone sank more than 50 French sailing-ships, with the result that after the war France did not build any more windjammers. Thus a great seafaring nation disappeared from the group of those still operating fleets under sail. In order to provide work for its expanding heavy industry, Britain now relied exclusively on building steamships and the newly developed diesel-powered motor vessels. Most of the German windjammers were divided up among the victorious nations, as part of the postwar reparation payments. With a stubborn devotion to tradition, Carl Laeisz' son Erich succeeded in gradually buying back the majority of these ships, including the PAMIR and the PASSAT. He used them to continue carrying guano and saltpetre from South America and wheat from Australia.

Even before the First World War, the German chemist Fritz Haber had discovered that it was possible to fix

The four-masted barque PAMIR *(right)*, built in 1905, sank in 1957. The PADUA was launched in 1926 and, after the Second World War, she was converted into a sail training-ship by the Russians, who renamed her KRUZENSHTERN.

nitrogen by synthesising nitrogen from the air with hydrogen under high pressure, to produce ammonia. During the war, when the high demand for nitrogen for explosives and fertilisers became a problem for the German empire, cut off from imported sources, Haber, in collaboration with Carl Bosch, succeeded in introducing the Haber-Bosch ammonia synthesis process into the German nitrogen industry. An industrially produced substitute for guano and saltpetre had been found, and the Chilean trade lost its economic justification. Nonetheless, Erich Laeisz, loyal to the windjammer tradition, ordered a new four-masted vessel in 1926. The magnificent PADUA was the last great sailing-ship to be launched. Steam- and motor-driven ships had won the battle, and the remaining sailing-ships could only be sold off for their scrap value.

This was the moment for the Finnish ship-owner, Gustaf Erikson, to take the stage. At bargain-basement prices ranging from £1,500 to £5,000 sterling, his shipping company, based at the port of Mariehamn in the Aaland Islands, bought up most of the big sailing-ships that were still afloat. Erikson sent them out to ply the seas again, but now on penny-pinching budget. He could only make a commercial profit from this by not insuring his ships, and by taking an initial deposit from his crewmen, which was

PASSAT
PASSAT

The PASSAT *(left)* and her sister-ship PEKING were launched in Hamburg in 1911. Both four-masted barques survived the war and many storms. The PASSAT is the last P-line ship in Germany. She lies in the Baltic, off Travemünde near Lübeck, as a maritime museum and a meeting centre for international youth. The PEKING is moored at the quayside in New York's South Street Seaport.

repaid gradually from their meagre wage. The fact that he could find any men willing to work so hard on these terms was due in part to German maritime law, which made the completion of two years in sailing-ships obligatory for obtaining a master's certificate. Prospective ship's officers completed their training on the sail training-ships that were now being commissioned everywhere. It had not been forgotten that there was no better place to learn team spirit and an understanding of the forces of nature than on a big sailing-ship. So it was that a number of windjammers found their last and by no means worst vocation in the training of young seamen.

Even after the Second World War a few of Erikson's windjammers continued to sail the seas like lonely ghost-ships with cargoes of timber, grain and guano. Then, on 21 August 1957, the one-time Laeisz windjammer PAMIR, now a German sail training-ship, was heading back across the Atlantic from Buenos Aires with a cargo of wheat, when she was caught in a hurricane. She broached to, the cargo shifted and she finally capsized. Of the 86-man crew, only 6 were saved, in one of the most costly and dangerous rescue operations in maritime history. At a position of latitude 36° N and longitude 40° W, the 6000-year history of mercantile sailing in the western hemisphere finally came to an end. Most of the remaining windjammers were destined for the ship-breaker's yard. But a few lucky ones escaped this fate and headed for their final berth as museum-ships, like the PASSAT in Travemünde, near Lübeck, the RICKMERS in Hamburg, the PEKING in New York or the POMMERN in Erikson's home port of Mariehamn. It was the sight of them as a young boy that began a great dream for the ship-owner Mikael Krafft: to resurrect the age of the clippers and windjammers…

RACING THE WIND

Schooners are the birds of the sea, whose swimming is like flying, and resemblesmore a natural function than the handling of man-invented appliances.

JOSEPH CONRAD , *THE MIRROR OF THE SEA*

Since time immemorial ships have been employed not merely for the transport of people and goods, or for purposes of war, but have also served man's leisure. Cleopatra sailed on the Nile in her galea, purely for amusement. As an early Dutch text tells us, sailing-ships were built for »business of state, transport of freight or simply for the pleasure of the passengers who travelled in them.« The last group have been described since the middle of the 16 th century as »yachts«. This term first appears in 1551 in the *Histoire de la Marine Française* and has its roots in the German word *»Jagd«*, meaning »hunt« or »pursuit«. The English later took up the word and gave it the meaning it still has today, namely to define any boat solely used for pleasure.

It was the Dutch who, having grown rich through trade in the 17th century, first had boats built for their own enjoyment. Their yachts were beamy vessels, which drew little and could easily navigate the shallow coastal waters. To compensate for the lack of a keel they had retractable lee-boards to prevent them drifting downwind, a feature still seen today. Their extravagant decoration and gilding proclaimed the wealth of their owners. As far back as 1622 a harbour exclusively for yachts was opened in Amsterdam, and two more would follow within twenty years.

It was of course the sport-obsessed British, who turned a leisurely pastime into a competitive activity. In 1660 wealthy Amsterdam merchants of the East India Company had cannily made a gift of the yacht MARY to King Charles II on his visit to the Netherlands. The single-masted vessel, 26 metres (85 ft) long, was rigged with a gaff mainsail and foresails, and fitted with lee-boards. Elaborate gilding decorated the transom stern and the gunports for its cannons. The partly gilded interior was no less luxurious. Thus the MARY set the standard for all future royal yachts. Sad to relate, in 1675 she sank in a storm in the Irish Sea off Holyhead. She lies there still and was located in 1973.

The sailing-mad Charles II had no fewer than 28 further yachts built, and raced them against each other on the Thames. These contests were given the name »regatta« from a word in Venetian dialect meaning the start-line of a rowing race. The first historically attested regatta, at which a prize of £100 was offered to the winner, took place in 1661 and ran from Greenwich – on the Thames a few miles below London – downstream to Gravesend and back.

»All hands on deck!«
»Sailing is misery and sailing is bliss, sailing is rain and sailing is sun. Sailing is wind and foaming waves, sailing is the coast, an anchorage, time to dream ...«

The winner was the yacht CATHERINE, with the King himself on board, and not above lending a royal hand to trim the sails. While regattas of this kind remained the preserve of royalty for the next century, the less sporty royal court of France mocked the caprice of the English by launching miniature copies of their yachts in the artificial lake at Versailles. So Louis XIV had his races too, without ever getting wet. Though France is a great maritime nation, it was relatively late in embracing the regatta. Not until 1841 was the first French yacht-club, the *Société des Régates du Havre*, established in France's principal Atlantic seaport.

However, the first yacht-club recorded anywhere in the world was Irish. The Water Club of the Harbour of Cork was founded in 1720, though its activities were certainly more social than sporting. The 25 members met every fortnight for a lavish dinner, at which the Admiral of the club had to provide a bottle of wine for each member. The first yacht-club in the United Kingdom was the Royal Thames Yacht Club, founded in London in 1775. But it was earlier, in 1749, that two »commoners«, in other words lesser nobility not related to the Royal Family, were allowed to compete for a trophy by racing from Greenwich

to the Nore headland, thus breaking the royal privilege. Since the Thames had thus ceased to be a princely preserve - and probably also due to the growth of waterborne traffic on its lower reaches – the royals transferred their yachting activities to Cowes on the Isle of Wight, where in 1815 the Yacht Club of Cowes was born. Its name was later changed to the Royal Yacht Squadron, and still in its original premises at the mouth of Cowes harbour, it is today considered the most exclusive yacht-club of them all.

The following extract from the Club Rules gives an insight into the formalities governing behaviour: »Although many members of this Club are unknown to each other, it is desirable that they render each other assistance in an emergency, even if they have not been introduced.« Ever since 1826, the Cowes Week regatta, held annually in mid-August, has remained as much of a fixture in the society calendar as the horse-racing at Ascot.

When Queen Victoria's grandson, Kaiser Wilhelm II, visited Cowes Week, the navy-mad German emperor decided to establish something similar. In the Baltic port of Kiel he not only founded the Imperial Yacht Club, but matched Cowes Week with the *Kieler Woche* in June. In 1906 he added the spice of a transatlantic race for the Kaiser's Cup. This race is no longer held, but Kiel Week is a regular fixture in the international sailing season. Admittedly, the leading position of Cowes Week could never be challenged, since Cowes was and remains the Mecca for all sailing enthusiasts. It is said that in the waters of the Solent – the stretch of water between the Isle of Wight and the south coast of England – every important advance in sail technology has its origin, from the replacement of traditional hemp shrouds with galvanised wire, to the invention of the spinnaker. It is from here, too, that the Admiral's Cup starts – today still the most famous and challenging yacht-race of all, which has now developed into a contest between international crews. The world's longest and most spectacular sailing contest, the 27,000- mile Whitbread Round-the-World Race, renamed the Volvo Ocean Race since 2002, also begins in the waters of the Solent.

These names signal a complete change in blue-water yachting. If this expensive pastime was initially open only to privileged members of royal and noble families, then later to the financial aristocracy of America's eastern seaboard, it has now, in the media age, become a hugely

Among all the ropes, every one has its proper place. Whether it be a towing-warp as thick as your arm, a sheet, a wire hauser, lifeline, seizing or buntline – with so many names and functions, the rigging of a big sailing-ship leaves the landlubber in a state of confusion.

more costly and spectacular sport, which is today sponsored by major companies and practised by highly-paid professionals. The British brewing-firm of Whitbread started by lending its name to the race; now Volvo has taken it over.

The boats that line up for the start here have as much in common with the yachts of yore as Formula-1 racing-cars have with Henry Ford's »Tin Lizzie«. All comfort on board is sacrificed to the need to save weight. For just that reason, in the 2002-3 Volvo Ocean Race, won by the German ILLBRUCK CHALLENGE with her skipper John Kostecki, the crew members were allowed to take only one pair of socks on each lap of the race. New light but super-strong materials have revolutionised hull construction and sailing gear. In many areas of navigation, the yachtsmen need only read data off the instruments of reliable but user-friendly electronic systems. Nevertheless, ocean racing is still far from lacking danger and adventure. One need only mention here the Fastnet Race of 1979, part of the Admiral's Cup competition, when a storm rose unexpectedly in the Irish Sea and claimed the lives of 15 participants. Anyone who remembers seeing the gripping images from the on-board cameras in the Volvo Ocean Race as the yachts rounded Cape Horn in heavy seas, knows only too well that the elements have lost none of their violence and terror.

The history of modern yacht-racing has been decisively influenced by the United States, which is no surprise since, after all, the prototype of all contemporary yacht design – the schooner – was an American invention. To sail in their shallow coastal waters with many river estuaries, the Americans needed ships that were fast and nimble, and which were also able to beat to windward well. For this reason, instead of the customary square rig, they used fore-and-aft sails with a long gaff at the head and boom at the foot. In order to achieve a straight, slender line, they did away with the »forecastle« and »stern-castle« and predicated the entire ship on the factors of speed and manoeuvrability. Derived from slavers' and smugglers' ships, schooners were employed at first as pilot-boats. Speed was of the essence, since the first pilot to reach an incoming vessel got the job. Subsequently, the customs and coast-guard used the fast vessels, known as »revenue cutters« and usually rigged with three masts, to chase smugglers and pirates. Finally, the financial and industrial barons of the East Coast found in the schooner a source of prestigious leisure enjoyment.

The Boston Boat Club, founded in 1830, was the first yacht-club in the USA, and it was open to anyone who could afford to pay for the sport. Fourteen years later, John Cox Stevens, scion of a family that had made its fortune from the railroads, created what is probably the most famous of all sailing-clubs, the New York Yacht Club. The clubhouse with its façade copied from the magnificent stern of a galleon, still stands on a Fifth Avenue site donated by J.P.Morgan. Today, between soaring towers of steel and glass, it looks like the relic of a forgotten era. A few years ago a trophy disappeared from one of its rooms, having hitherto remained there unmolested for over a hundred years; it was an ugly silver pot with no bottom, but its symbolic value was of the very highest order: the America's Cup.

John Cox Stevens built himself a two-masted schooner purely for racing purposes. It had absolutely no luxury fittings and was designed solely for ease of handling by a small crew. In the AMERICA he crossed the Atlantic in 1851 to compete for the One Hundred Guinea Cup at the Cowes regatta. The course took them round the Isle of Wight in a clockwise direction, i.e. starting eastward. Stevens' crew and their professional skipper, Dick Brown, got off to a bad start, but in seamanship they quickly showed their superiority over the British, whose sails were still made from loose-woven hemp canvas that let through a lot of wind, whereas Stevens had machine-sewn, wind-tight sails made from cotton. Stevens took the trophy back to the USA in triumph. It was 19 years before the British dared to try and bring it home again. As recently as 1983, Alan Bond with his AUSTRALIA II, was the first non-American to win the Cup. A new era had begun.

Like all great yacht-races the America's Cup has become a media spectacle that swallows enormous sums of money (investments of over £40 million /US$60 million by each participant are not unusual). That is why the yachts can only be financed by sponsorship syndicates. The internationally selected crews are made up of highly-paid and high-performing sportsmen and specialists. Even so, there still remains a little spark of intuition, since even the most accurate instruments can only tell the skipper the present wind direction, not where it *will* be blowing from in a little while. That is something he still has to sense with his nose. And someone with that kind of nose can still become a big star today. For the more technology reduces the human

Without seamen's knots nothing can get done on a sailing-ship. If you want, you can get a sailor to show you the tricky bowline – or the clove hitch, the reef-knot, the sheet-bend the sheepshank, the monkey's fist or the Turk's head – whichever it is, it'll need practice, practice, practice...

factor, the more vital that factor becomes where it *cannot* be replaced by technology.

The original yacht-racing spirit can still be captured in the annual Antigua Classic Yacht Regatta, in which any classic long-keeled yachts can take part – sloops, cutters, yawls, ketches, brigs, brigantines, barquentines and other square-rigged or fore-and-aft rigged vessels, be they renovated originals, or recently built replicas. And anyone who thinks this might have the cosy atmosphere of a vintage car rally, is seriously mistaken, as he will soon realise when he looks at the blisters on his hands after the first day's racing.

The victories of the STAR CLIPPER in the big sailing-ship class, the Tall Ships World Peace Cup, part of the annual Antigua Classic Yacht Regatta, confirm the superb sailing qualities of these vessels – and of course also the ability of her crew to sail fast with the sporting »hands-on« passengers. This regatta forms part of the cruise programme.

THE SEA – UNBOUNDED IN ITS FASCINATION

Nothing can touch the brooding bitterness of its heart…
To love it is not well. It knows no bond of plighted troth,
no fidelity to misfortune, to long companionship, to devotion.

JOSEPH CONRAD, *THE MIRROR OF THE SEA*

Sailing today is a leisure pastime and a high-performance sport. And yet the wind that is caught by the kevlar-reinforced, high-tech designed mainsail of an America's Cup yacht, is the same wind that 6,000 years ago blew the tattered sail of a felucca on the Nile. That sail was hung from a pole on the papyrus-built craft, as a means of propulsion; it is the ancient dream of mastering the forces of nature without doing violence to nature itself. With the renaissance of the old clippers and windjammers, this dream has taken concrete shape again. Playing with wind is a two-way game: the seafarer masters it, yet at the same time he is at its mercy, either because of its absence or of its great power. Knowledge of tides and currents enables us to calculate the best course. Sailing makes people cunning. When travelling by air we are accustomed to regarding distance purely in terms of time. Florida is 10 hours away, not 6,000 miles. Sailing makes us once again see distance as a measure of space. And this gives us a sense of wellbeing, since it corresponds to our organic perception of the world. It was in sailing-ships that mankind gained the first, rough overview of the planet on which we live. Those who sailed the seas could describe the world, and those like James Cook, who looked more closely, could even explain it in part. The great sailing-ships of the 16th to 19th centuries were instruments of discovery, to be followed only later by vessels of transportation. That is the origin of their myth, and it is something we still feel instinctively today when we come across them, either as restored museum exhibits or fully functioning replicas.

Sailing sharpens the senses. Waves must be watched, the wind obeyed, the spicy waft of approaching land savoured in the air, a change of wind sniffed, the tension of a sail felt in the hand. Seamen are known for their taciturnity. That is why authors with a love of the sea, like Conrad or Hemingway, have cultivated a style distinguished by the absence of any superfluous words. And that is also why I leave the final words to the British author and poet of the

sea, John Masefield. In his book *Hurricane, the Story of a Rescue,* we find all the sensual power that the sea can give to a gifted writer:

»Then suddenly the roaring to windward became deeper, turned into an burst of thunder, worse than all the raging up till then. Long before it was upon them, they heard it and felt their blood freeze. It was like an explosion all around them. The mountain of water, which had been towering above them, hit the ship as though a gigantic beam was crashing on to it. The ship heeled heavily under the blow and shook itself like a wounded beast that walks even as it is dying. Only then did the hurricane make its violent entrance.

It seemed impossible that this impact could actually be wind. Some cataclysm must have shaken the planet. Yet it was wind. But what had created it? From how far had it come? How much further would it race? What could halt it or bring it to an end? It was wind, air in motion, nothing more. Birds had flown in it, men had breathed it, one day it would be air once again, but at that moment it was the breath of death.

It gradually grew lighter, although the whole sky in the north and partly in the east as well was still black and overcast from the swirling smoke of the hurricane.

The radiant orb of the sun rose up from the clutches of the sea. It made a glittering path across the water and cast its light on the exhausted men. As it lifted itself from the horizon it bathed the pewter columns of the sea in beauty. In its valleys the sea was blue once more, its crests were green and like snow on the breakers; and when the men now looked for the storm, they saw it like an island low on the horizon, with bands of smoke above it. The uppermost waves of smoke were like cumulus clouds that presage a storm; they had a coppery glow, and swelled slowly upwards like balloons being inflated from below. As the sun rose higher, they took on a pale, reddish colour, then cooled to a dazzling white so that they overtopped the sea like the cordilleras under fresh snow.«

Aback (prep.) with the wind dead ahead, stopping the ship
Abaft (prep.) behind, to the rear of
Abeam (prep.) at right angles to the ship and at a distance. E.g »Cape Horn is abeam«
About (prep.) to »go about« or »put a vessel about« means to swing the bow into and across the wind, so that the sails then fill on the other side. (see also: »tack«)
Aft (prep.) towards the stern or rear of a ship e.g. »all hands aft«
After (adj.) describes an object that is »aft« of something else, e.g. »the after bulkhead«
Apparent wind (n.) The direction of the wind as perceived on board, altered by the forward motion of the ship and therefore coming from a point closer to the bow.
Astern (prep.) backwards, or behind. E.g. »Slow astern«, »the ship is astern of us«
Back (vb. trans.) to pull or swing a sail towards the wind in order to stop or change course quickly, as in »back the jib«
Back (vb. intrans.) the wind »backs« when it changes direction contrary to the sun's movement (see also: Veer)
Backstay (n.) see »stay«
Barque (n.) sailing-ship with at least three masts, of which the two forward ones are square-rigged. (fig.12)
Barquentine (n.) (Star Clipper) sailing-ship with three or more masts of which only the foremast is square-rigged.(fig.11)
Bearing (n.) angle of view to a distant object, defined in degrees from north (e.g »bearing 45°«) or as a compass-point (e.g »bearing north-east«)
Beat (vb.) (to windward) to sail at the closest possible angle to the wind
Beat (n.) the point of sailing described above, as opposed to a »reach« or a »run« (q.v.)
Beaufort Scale (n.) standard measure of wind, from Force 1 (light air) through Force 5 (fresh breeze, 17-21 knots) to 8 (gale, 34-40 knots) and 12 (hurricane, over 64 knots)
Belay (vb.) to make fast (tie or fasten) a rope that is under tension
Belaying-pin (n.) a vertical wooden or metal peg to which ropes are tied (usually figure-of-eight fashion)
Bell (n.) the ship's bell is »sounded« on the hour and half-hour and to signify a change of watch
Bermuda rig (n.) modern form of fore-and-aft rig, in which the mainsail and mizzen have no gaff (q.v.) but taper to a point near the masthead.
Bilges (n.) spaces at the very bottom of the hull, in which sea-water often collects
Block (n.) an oval-shaped piece of wood or metal that houses one or more pulley-wheels, through which ropes are run.
Block-and-tackle (n.) combination of two or more blocks and ropes to assist in pulling or hoisting a heavy load
Boatswain (n.) (pronounced »bo-sun«), Officer or senior seaman in charge of sails and rigging
Boom (n.) in fore-and-aft rig, a long wooden or metal spar that holds the foot of a sail
Bow (n.) the front end or nose of a ship
Bowsprit (n.) on older sailing ships and yachts, a wooden spar protruding beyond the bow to carry foresails
Brace (n.) rope used to swing a yard-arm (q.v.) horizontally on the mast.
Brace (vb.) to pull the brace and swing the yard-arm (to catch the wind)
Breakwater (n.) stone-built wall separating a harbour from the sea.
Breeze wind of up to moderate strength; described as light, fresh or stiff
Bridge on larger vessels, the raised position from which officers give orders
Brigantine (n.) Two-masted ship, in which only the foremast is square-rigged (fig.9)
Brig (n.) Two-masted ship, in which both masts are square-rigged (fig.10)
Bulkhead (n.) strong transverse wall below deck in a ship
Bulwark (n.) Solid wooden or metal barrier round the edge of the deck, to prevent people falling overboard
Bunk (n.) narrow, box-like bed on a ship, often built in tiers
Buntlines (n.) On square-riggers, ropes used to haul the body of the sail up on to the yard-arm for furling.
Check (vb.) to slacken, e.g. »check jib sheet«
Classic yacht (n.) yacht with a single deep keel, rudder mounted directly behind the keel, and traditional rig. Must be constructed of wood or steel, not plastic
Clew (n.) in fore-and-aft rig, the bottom, after corner of a sail, to which the sheet (q.v.) is attached)
Clipper (n.) sailing-ship built in the later 19th C. to carry light cargoes (esp. tea) at high speed
Compass (n.) Instrument with a freely rotating horizontal disc which always points to magnetic north. Used for navigation and taking bearings.
Counter-stern (n.) Design where the rear (stern) of the ship slopes inwards at an angle to the waterline. (see figs. 4 and 6)
Crow's nest (n.) Enclosed wooden structure high on the foremast, where the lookout sits
Cutter (n.) yacht with a single mast and bowsprit carrying at least two foresails (fig. 6)
Davits (n.) pair of curved arms at the ship's side, from which a lifeboat or ship's boat is suspended and can be quickly lowered.
Derrick small on-board crane for lifting cargo, provisions etc
Dodger (n.) protective canvas fitted above the bulwark or rail to deflect heavy spray
Figurehead (n.) Decoratively carved head and bust, often of a legendary character, and usually female, that adorns the stem-post of a traditional ship
Footline (n.) In square-riggers, ropes suspended below the yard-arms, on which sailors stand when furling the sails
Fore-and-aft sails, rig etc. (n.) sails or rig that run in the bow-to-stern direction, as opposed to »square rig« with its transverse spars
Forecastle (fo'c'sle): accommodation nearest the bow
Foredeck (n.) deck forward of the mainmast or foremast
Foremast (n.) forward mast of a multi-masted ship, or of a 2-masted schooner
Forepeak (n.) space below deck in the very bow of a ship for stowage or ballast
Furl (vb.) to bundle a square-sail on its yard-arm
Flake down (vb.) to fold a fore-and-aft sail tidily on to its boom or the deck
Gaff (n.) Wooden spar holding the head of a mainsail or mizzen in fore-and-aft rig. It is hauled up with the sail from the deck.
Gaff-rigged (adj.) describing the traditional form of fore-and-aft rig, using gaffs.
Gaff cutter (n.) single-masted yacht, with gaff-rigged mainsail and jib rigged to the bowsprit. (fig.2)
Galley (n.) ship's kitchen
Gear (n.) term applied to all rigging and equipment; divided into »standing« (fixed) and »running« (movable) gear
Genoa jib (n.) large foresail rigged from the masthead to the stem, with the foot running well aft off the mainmast (see fig.3)
Gunwale (n.) the upper edge of a ship's side
Gybe (vb. and n.) To alter course, usually with the wind aft, so that the stern swings across the wind and the sails fill on the other side.
Halyard (n.) rope for hauling a sail up the mast
Hand (n.) any member of a crew
Heel (vb.) of a sailing vessel, to tilt under pressure from wind
Helmsman (n.) seaman who steers a vessel with the wheel or tiller
Hoist (vb.) to haul something up by rope, usually a sail or flag

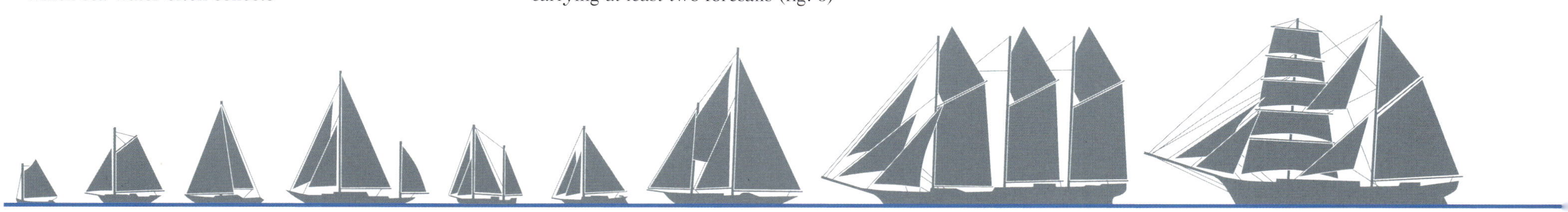

1 2 3 4 5 6 7 8 9

Horizon (n.) In clear visibility, the line where the sea »meets« the sky due to the earth's curvature.
»In irons« A sailing-ship is said to be »in irons« when the wind has come dead ahead and the ship is motionless, unable to swing either way to catch the wind
Jetty (n.) small wooden pier
Jib (n.) Small sail hoisted on the foremast and attached to the bow or bowsprit.
Keel (n.) The lowest longitudinal timbers and narrow, underwater section of a ship's hull
Ketch (n.) Two-masted sailing-vessel, in which the after or mizzen-mast is located forward of the rudder-post (fig. 5)
Knot (n.) Measurement of a ship's speed: 1 knot = 1 nautical mile (q.v.) per hour. The name »knot« comes from the traditional ship's log-line, with knots at intervals, for measuring speed.
Leech (n.) in fore-and-aft rig, the trailing vertical edge of a sail
Lee, leeward (n., adj.) denotes anything on the side of the ship away from the wind; »in the lee« of something means protected by it from the wind. (opposite of »windward«)
List (vb., n.) Of any vessel, to tilt for a reason other than wind, e.g. because it is taking water, or the cargo has shifted
Log (n.) 1.ship's journal in which all occurrences and navigational data are entered
2. Apparatus for measuring ship's speed or distance covered (either electronic, mechanical or manual i.e. a knotted line paid out and timed)
Luff (n.) in fore-and-aft rig, the forward edge of a sail
Luff (vb.) to swing the ship's head into the wind
Lugger (n.) small boat with mast stepped far forward and a single gaff-rigged sail (fig.1)
Mate (n.) as in »first mate«, experienced seaman with responsibility over others
Midships 1. (n.) Central position of steering-wheel, as in »helm a-midships«). 2. (n.) middle section of the ship
Mizzen (n.) small sail in the stern (q.v.) of the ship
Mizzen-mast (n) short mast in the stern that carries the mizzen.
Mole (n.) solid, stone-built pier
Monsoon (n.) seasonal tropical wind that blows across the Indian Ocean from the south-west in summer, carrying heavy rain into south Asia; in winter, a dry wind blowing in the opposite direction
Nautical day (n.) 24 hours counted from noon to noon
Nautical mile (n.) defined as the distance on the earth's surface subtended by an angle of 1 minute of latitude at the centre of the earth: 6,080 ft (1,852 m.)
Pilot (n.) shore-based expert on local navigation, who comes aboard to take a ship into harbour or through a difficult channel
Port (n.), adj. left hand side of a ship, facing the bow. Denoted by the colour red.
Porthole (n.) Small, strong, circular window in the ship's side
Reach (vb., n.) to sail with the wind at about 90° to the ship's direction; this is called »a broad reach«
Reef (n.) long underwater rock formation, close to the surface
Reef (vb.) to reduce the size of a sail in strong wind, by rolling or folding and tying it,
Regatta (n.) series of organised rowing or sailing races spread over one or more days
Rig (n.) arrangement of masts and sails in a certain configuration
Rigger (n.) seaman who fixes and maintains the rigging
Roads or roadstead (n.) safe, sheltered anchorage outside a harbour
Roller-jib (n.) On modern yachts, a foresail that can be furled by rolling it up on the forestay
Run (vb., n.) to sail with the wind roughly behind the ship
Schooner (n.) Fore-and-aft rigged sailing-vessel with two or more masts, in which the foremast is same height or lower than the other(s) (figs. 7 and 8)
Scupper (n.) shallow channel running round the edge of the deck to drain away water
Sextant (n.) navigational instrument to measure the angle of elevation of the sun or a star from the horizon
Shackle (n.) U-shaped steel piece on the end of a rope, sail etc, which is closed with a bar (»pin«) that is screwed or clipped in position, and attached to some other fitting
Shanty (n.) rhythmic seamen's song to help with tasks such as hauling in the anchor
Sheet (n.) in fore-and-aft rig, a rope attached to the outer bottom corner of a sail, or its boom, to control its angle to the wind
Shroud (n.) Strong fixed rigging either side of a mast, to support it.
Skipper (n.) someone with a certificate qualifying him or her to take charge of a yacht or larger sailing-vessel
Sloop (n.) single-masted yacht with no bowsprit and a single large foresail
Soldier's wind (n.) good steady breeze blowing from the stern quarter
Spar (n.) long piece of wood such as the boom, gaff or yard-arm, that holds a sail when set
Square rig (n.) traditional rig in which square sails are supported on yard-arms (q.v.) attached to the mast. The yards can be swung round to about 45° to the centre-line of the ship. Opposite of fore-and-aft rig.
Square-rigger (n.) sailing-ship with two or more masts and square, transverse sails
Standing rigging (n.) fixed ropes and wires that support the masts, principally the shrouds and stays
Starboard (n., adj.) right hand side of a ship, facing the bow. Denoted by the colour green
Stay (n.) strong fixed rope or wire supporting a mast from the front (forestay) and rear (backstay)
Staysail (n.) 1. Foresail that is set between the jib and the main- or forem. 2. Triangular sail set between the masts of 2-masted schooner (fig.7)
Stern (n.) rear end of a ship or boat
Swell (n.) long-waved motion of the sea that continues over considerable distances and is not directly influenced by the local wind.
Tack (vb.) to sail on a zigzag course against the wind, about 40° to the wind on either side
Tack (n.) each leg of the zig-zag; starboard tack is with wind from starboard side etc.
Tackle (n.) general term for all ropes and other movable gear on a ship
Tender (n.) small boat, usually motor-powered, to carry people between ship and shore
Tiller (n.) on smaller yachts and dinghies, a wooden arm attached to the rudder for steering
Topsail schooner (n.) schooner with mainsails and topsails, both gaff-rigged (fig.8)
Trade-winds (n.) constant winds that blow from the NE towards the equator, roughly from the latitude 30° N, and from the SE towards the equator from latitude 30° S.
Trim (vb.) to adjust the tension and angle of sails in order to maximise their driving force
Typhoon (n.) tropical hurricane occurring in the western Pacific
Veer (vb.) the wind »veers« when it changes direction parallel to the sun's movement
Watch (n.) regular 4-hour spell of duty on deck
Windward (adj., prep.) denotes anything on the side of the ship nearest the wind, or in the direction from which the wind is coming; sailing or beating to windward means sailing at the closest angle possible to the wind
Yard, yard-arm (n.) horizontal spar attached to the mast, from which sales hang in a square-rigged ship
Yawl (n.) two-masted yacht, with a mainmast and small mizzen stepped as far aft as possible (fig.4)

10

11

12

13

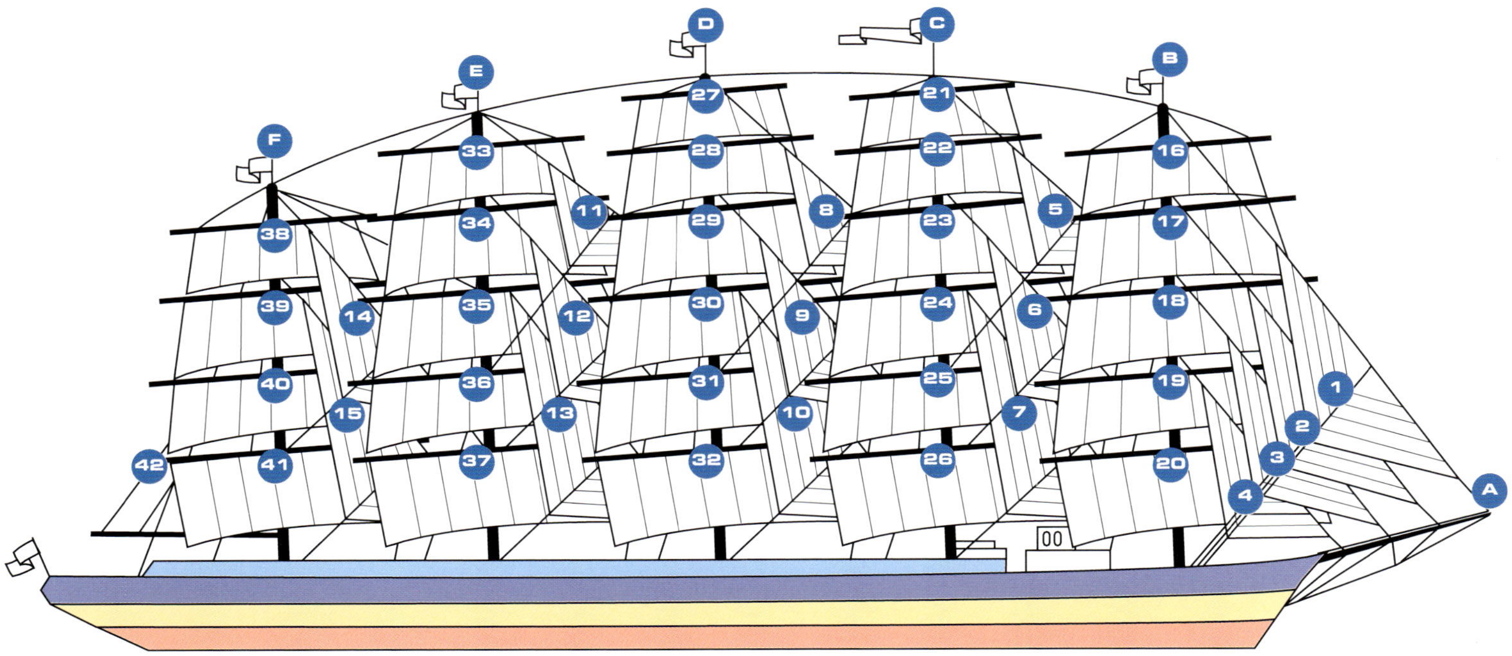

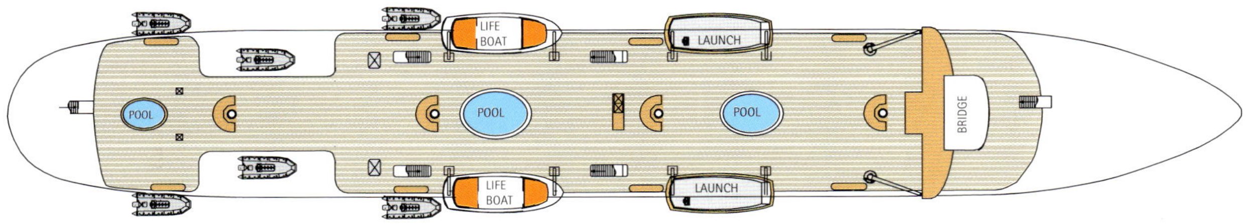

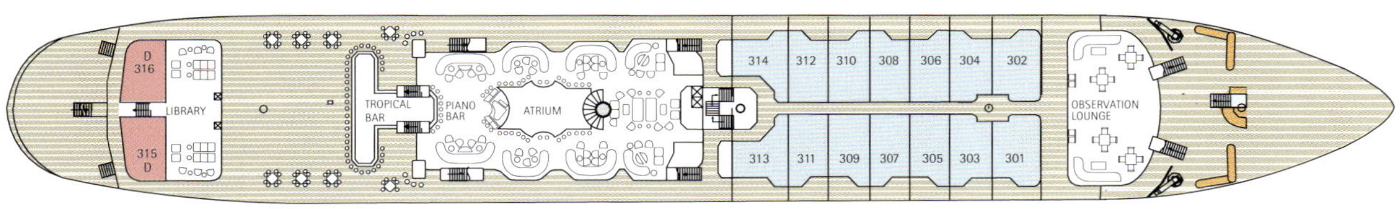

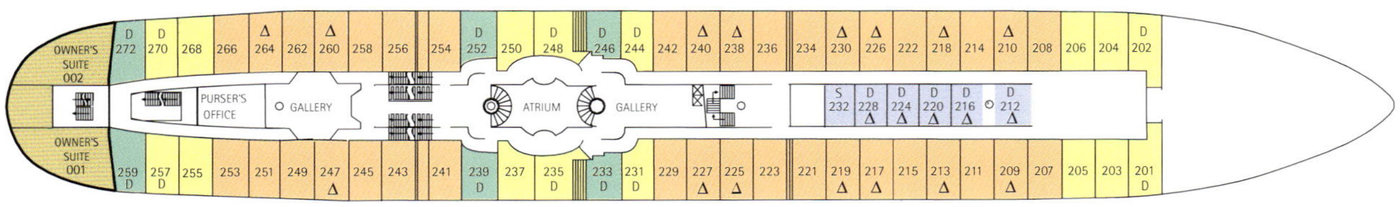

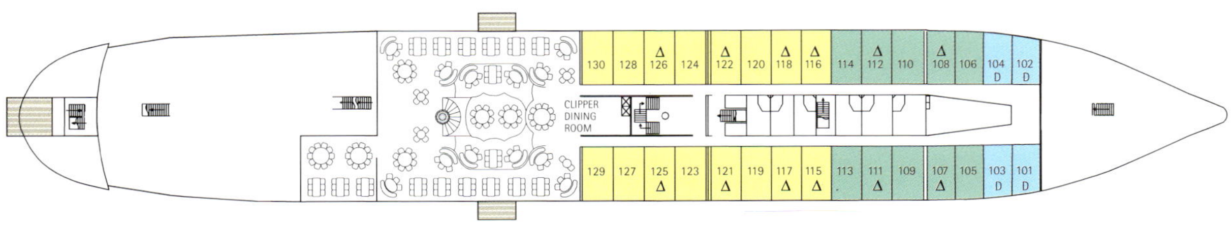

Technical data:
Tonnage: 5,050
Length: 134 m. (440 ft)
Beam: 16.5m (54 ft)
Draught: 5.6m (18 ft 4in)
Sail-area: 5,000 sq.m
Mast height: 54m (177 ft)
5 masts, 42 sails
Crew: 100
Passenger capacity: 227

Plan of masts and sails

A Bowsprit
B Foremast
C Mainmast
D Middle-mast
E After-mast
F Mizzen-mast
1 Flying-jib
2 Outer jib
3 Inner jib
4 Fore-topmast staysail
5 Main royal staysail
6 Main topgallant staysail
7 Main staysail
8 Middle royal staysail
9 Middle topgallant staysail
10 Middle staysail
11 After royal staysail
12 After topgallant staysail
13 After staysail
14 Mizzen topgallant staysail
15 Mizzen staysail
16 Upper fore topgallant sail
17 Lower fore topgallant sail
18 Upper fore topsail
19 Lower fore topsail
20 Foresail
21 Main royal
22 Upper main topgallant
23 Lower main topgallant
24 Upper main topsail
25 Lower main topsail
26 Mainsail
27 Middle royal
28 Upper middle topgallant
29 Lower middle topgallant
30 Upper middle topsail
31 Lower middle topsail
32 Middle sail
33 Upper after topgallant
34 Lower after topgallant
35 Upper after topsail
36 Lower after topsail
37 After-sail
38 Mizzen topgallant
39 Upper mizzen topsail
40 Lower mizzen topsail
41 Mizzen or crossjack
42 Spanker

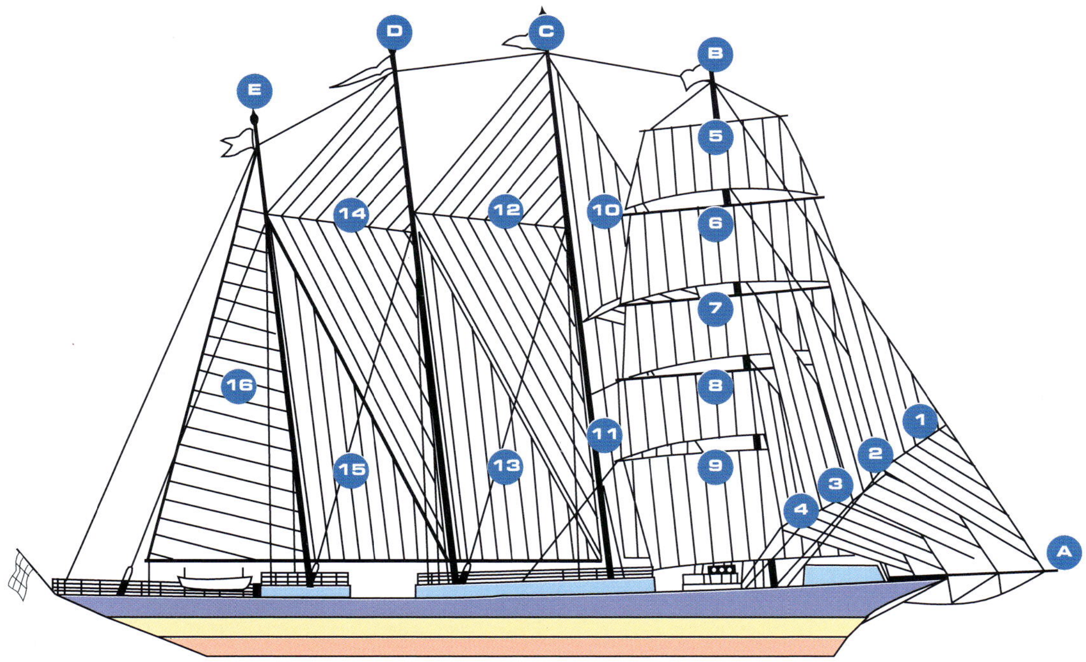

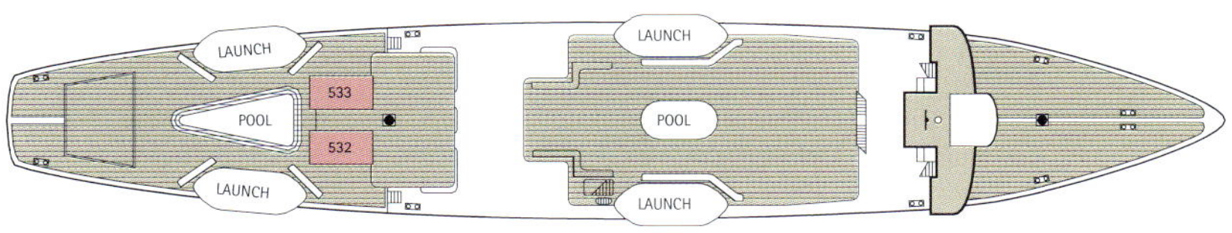

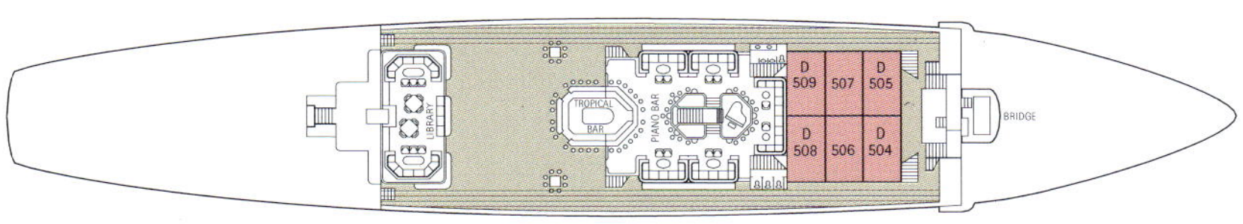

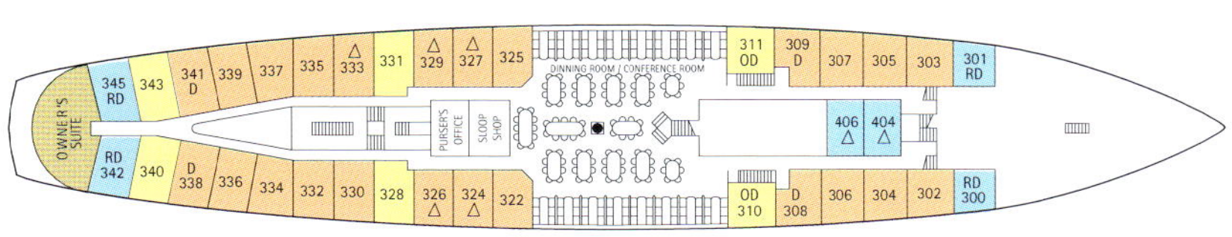

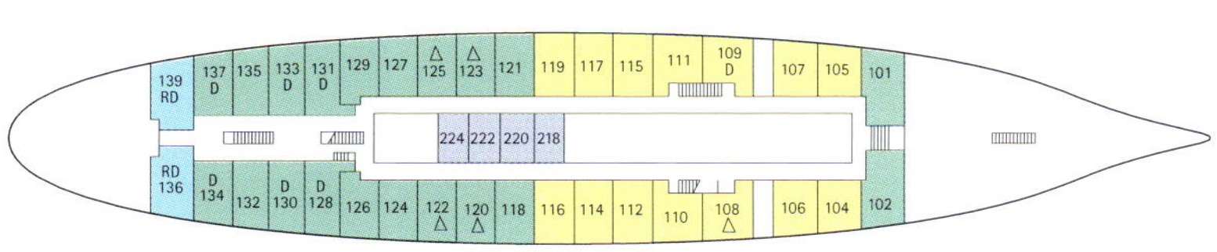

Technical data
Length: 115.5m (379 ft)
Beam: 15m (49 ft)
Sail-area: 3,365 sq.m
Engine: 12 cylinder
Single propeller
Caterpillar diesel
Crew: 70
Passenger capacity: 170

Mast- und Segelplan

A Bowsprit
B Foremast
C Mainmast
D After-mast
E Mizzen-mast
1 Flying-jib
2 Outer jib
3 Inner jib
4 Staysail
5 Upper topgallant
6 Lower topgallant
7 Upper topsail
8 Lower topsail
9 Foresail
10 Main topgallant
11 Main staysail
12 Main »fisherman«
13 After staysail
14 After »fisherman«
15 Mizzen staysail
16 Mizzen

The is company house-flag represents the »big yacht« atmosphere and hands-on sailing adventure – that is the guiding principle by which all the ships in the Star Clipper fleet operate.

Picture credits

Deutsches Schifffahrtsmuseum,
(German Maritime Museum) Bremerhaven:
138, 140, 142 (below)
Ullstein Bild:
128, 142 (above), 145 (left); 145(right: Ullstein Bild / dpa),
146 (Ullstein Bild / Schlemmer)

All other photographs were taken by Michael Friedel

Impressum

DSV Deutscher Sportverlag GmbH
Frankenwerft 35
50667 Cologne, Germany

Text on pages 28-120: Marion Friedel
Design: Michael Stahl, Munich
Repro: Franzi's print & media, Munich
Printed by: Klingenberg Buchkunst Leipzig

ISBN: 3 - 937630-05-8

Printed in Germany 2004